ELECTRIC UTILITIES
AND
INDEPENDENT POWER:

IMPACT OF DEREGULATION

ELECTRIC UTILITIES
AND
INDEPENDENT POWER:
IMPACT OF DEREGULATION

by
Richard K. Miller, CEM

Published by
THE FAIRMONT PRESS, INC.
700 Indian Trail
Lilburn, GA 30247

Library of Congress Cataloging-in-Publication Data

Miller, Richard Kendall, 1946-
  Electric utilities and independent power : impact of deregulation / by
Richard K. Miller.
  p. cm.
  Includes bibliographical references.
  ISBN 0-88173-233-8
  1. Electric utilities--Deregulation--United States. 2. Competition--United
States. I. Title.
HD9685.U5M52   1995   333.79'32--dc20   95-22855
                                                      CIP

*Electric Utilities And Independent Power: Impact Of Deregulation / By
Richard K. Miller.*

Published by The Fairmont Press, Inc.
700 Indian Trail
Lilburn, GA 30247

Printed in the United States of America

10 9 8 7 6 5 4 3 2 1

ISBN 0-88173-233-8   FP

ISBN 0-13-520438-0   PH

While every effort is made to provide dependable information, the publisher, authors, and
editors cannot be held responsible for any errors or omissions.

Distributed by Prentice Hall PTR
Prentice-Hall, Inc.
A Simon & Schuster Company
Upper Saddle River, NJ 07458

Prentice-Hall International (UK) Limited, London
Prentice-Hall of Australia Pty. Limited, Sydney
Prentice-Hall Canada Inc., Toronto
Prentice-Hall Hispanoamericana, S.A., Mexico
Prentice-Hall of India Private Limited, New Delhi
Prentice-Hall of Japan, Inc., Tokyo
Simon & Schuster Asia Pte. Ltd., Singapore
Editora Prentice-Hall do Brasil, Ltda., Rio de Janeiro

TABLE OF CONTENTS

1 EXECUTIVE SUMMARY   1
  1.1 Trends and Market Assessment   1
  1.2 Recent Activities   2
  1.3 Short Term Outlook   4
  1.4 Mid-Range and Long Term Outlook   5
  1.5 Opportunities   7

2 DEREGULATION AND THE COMPETITIVE POWER MARKETPLACE   8
  2.1 Trends and Market Assessment   8
  2.2 Recent Activities   11
  2.3 Short Term Outlook   14
  2.4 Mid-Range and Long Term Outlook   14
  2.5 Opportunities   16

3 INVESTOR-OWNED ELECTRIC UTILITIES   18
  3.1 Trends and Market Assessment   18
  3.2 Recent Activities   20
  3.3 Short Term Outlook   22
  3.4 Mid-Range and Long Term Outlook   23
  3.5 Opportunities   26

4 INDEPENDENT POWER   28
  4.1 Trends and Market Assessment   28
  4.2 Recent Activities   29
  4.3 Short Term Outlook   31
  4.4 Mid-Range and Long Term Outlook   33
  4.5 Opportunities   34

5 THE ELECTRIC POWER MARKET   36
  5.1 Trends and Market Assessment   36
  5.2 Recent Activities   36
  5.3 Short Term Outlook   38
  5.4 Mid-Range and Long Term Outlook   39
  5.5 Opportunities   43

6 WHOLESALE WHEELING   44
  6.1 Trends and Market Assessment   44
  6.2 Recent Activities   46
  6.3 Short Term Outlook   48
  6.4 Mid-Range and Long Term Outlook   48
  6.5 Opportunities   49

7 RETAIL WHEELING 50
   7.1 Trends and Market Assessment 50
   7.2 Recent Activities 51
   7.3 Short Term Outlook 55
   7.4 Mid-Range and Long Term Outlook 56
   7.5 Opportunities 58

8 INTERNATIONAL ACTIVITIES 59
   8.1 Trends and Market Assessment 59
   8.2 Recent Activities 60
   8.3 Short Term Outlook 63
   8.4 Mid-Range and Long Term Outlook 65
   8.5 Opportunities 67

9 DEMAND-SIDE MANAGEMENT 69
   9.1 Trends and Market Assessment 69
   9.2 Recent Activities 71
   9.3 Short Term Outlook 76
   9.4 Mid-Range and Long Term Outlook 77
   9.5 Opportunities 78

10 ENERGY CONSERVATION EQUIPMENT AND SERVICES 81
   10.1 Trends and Market Assessment 81
   10.2 Recent Activities 86
   10.3 Short Term Outlook 90
   10.4 Mid-Range and Long Term Outlook 92
   10.5 Opportunities 94

11 POWER GENERATION CONSTRUCTION AND EQUIPMENT 96
   11.1 Trends and Market Assessment 96
   11.2 Recent Activities 97
   11.3 Short Term Outlook 101
   11.4 Mid-Range and Long Term Outlook 102
   11.5 Opportunities 106

12 TRANSMISSION AND DISTRIBUTION 108
   12.1 Trends and Market Assessment 108
   12.2 Recent Activities 109
   12.3 Short Term Outlook 112
   12.4 Mid-Range and Long Term Outlook 112
   12.5 Opportunities 114

13 FOSSIL FUEL GENERATION 115
   13.1 Trends and Market Assessment 115
   13.2 Recent Activities 116
   13.3 Short Term Outlook 120

13.4 Mid-Range and Long Term Outlook 120
13.5 Opportunities 128

14 NUCLEAR POWER 129
14.1 Trends and Market Assessment 129
14.2 Recent Activities 130
14.3 Short Term Outlook 133
14.4 Mid-Range and Long Term Outlook 135
14.5 Opportunities 137

15 HYDROELECTRIC 139
15.1 Trends and Market Assessment 139
15.2 Recent Activities 141
15.3 Short Term Outlook 141
15.4 Mid-Range and Long Term Outlook 143
15.5 Opportunities 144

16 BIOMASS AND WASTE-TO-ENERGY 147
16.1 Trends and Market Assessment 147
16.2 Recent Activities 149
16.3 Short Term Outlook 150
16.4 Mid-Range and Long Term Outlook 151
16.5 Opportunities 153

17 RENEWABLE ENERGY RESOURCES 155
17.1 Trends and Market Assessment 155
17.2 Recent Activities 157
17.3 Short Term Outlook 160
17.4 Mid-Range and Long Term Outlook 161
17.5 Opportunities 166

18 ENVIRONMENTAL ISSUES AND POLLUTION CONTROL 167
18.1 Trends and Market Assessment 167
18.2 Recent Activities 170
18.3 Short Term Outlook 174
18.4 Mid-Range and Long Term Outlook 174
18.5 Opportunities 175

19 ELECTRIC VEHICLES 176
19.1 Trends and Market Assessment 176
19.2 Recent Activities 177
19.3 Short Term Outlook 178
19.4 Mid-Range and Long Term Outlook 179
19.5 Opportunities 182

20 RATES   184
    20.1 Trends and Market Assessment   184
    20.2 Recent Activities   184
    20.3 Short Term Outlook   185
    20.4 Mid-Range and Long Term Outlook   186
    20.5 Opportunities   187

REFERENCES   189

1 EXECUTIVE SUMMARY

CONTENTS:

1.1 Trends and Market Assessment
1.2 Recent Activities
1.3 Short Term Outlook
1.4 Mid-Range and Long Term Outlook
1.5 Opportunities

1.1 Trends and Market Assessment

The United States spends roughly 7% of its $5.9 trillion Gross Domestic Product (GDP), or approximately $475 billion, on energy. Of this amount, approximately $175 billion is spent on electricity.

The U.S. electric utility industry is very diverse in terms of types and sizes of suppliers, regulatory requirements, and economic and customer characteristics. There are over 3,200 suppliers of electric energy in the United States, ranging from large investor-owned utilities to very small municipal systems. Some of these entities generate, transmit, and distribute electric power to customers, while others only distribute electric power generated by others.

The electric power generation business has undergone two momentous changes over the last decade. The most dramatic has been the deregulation and resulting competition in power generation. The independent power industry (i.e., non-utility generators) was born several years ago, however, it was the Energy Policy Act of 1992 that really opened up competition.

The electric power industry is rapidly becoming market-driven. This is a major change for an industry which, until the last decade, was characterized by large, vertically integrated monopolies. For some time, new powerplants have generally been subjects of competitive bidding. Now, with the implementation of open transmission access, wholesale markets are developing. Shortly, retail markets may follow, as California and other states propose or consider providing retail customers with the direct market access.

Air pollution control regulations have impacted utilities for more than two decades. The Clean Air Act Amendments of 1990 brought another round of challenge. Response from utilities include fuel switching, emission trading and the installation of air pollution control equipment. Concerns about global warming are now causing utilities to consider their carbon dioxide emissions. Potential health effects associated with exposure to electric and magnetic fields has emerged as a huge potential liability for utilities.

There have also been changes in power generation technology. There is a shift away from large coal-fired boiler steam systems to smaller natural gas-fired, combustion turbine-based systems. Fluidized bed boiler and clean coal technologies are also being utilized.

1.2 Recent Activities

The electric utility industry entered 1994 well aware of the challenges it faced. The issues of stranded investment and retail wheeling were primary among the challenges resulting from the Energy Policy Act of 1992 and the competitive market which is evolving. The 03 January 1994 issue of *Forbes* provided the following assessment from Standard & Poors, "For the first time ever, we have a negative outlook for the majority of the electric utility industry."

Indeed, 1994 was a year of challenge and change for the electric utility industry. Some of the major activities included:

- Several state public utility commissions initiated future plans for retail wheeling. The two major announcements were in California and Michigan, where specific schedules to implement or experiment with retail wheeling were promulgated.

- Power brokers and power marketers began to spring up throughout the United States and will assume a role as a major player in the new competitive power industry.

- Investor-owned utilities continued their cost-reduction and downsizing activities. This movement will place utilities in a stronger position to deal with the competitive marketplace which is rapidly emerging.

- The problem of stranded investment has emerged as the focal point of problems which may result from the deregulation brought about by the Energy Policy Act of 1992. In June 1994, the Federal Energy Regulatory Commission issued a proposed rulemaking which would serve as a framework for dealing with the recovery of stranded investments.

- Significant reductions were implemented in the demand-side management programs of several utilities, and others requested approval for cutbacks from public utility commissions.

- Independent power producers continued to garner an increasing share of the U.S. market for electrical power, but have begun to focus the majority of their new development efforts internationally, particularly in Asia and Latin America. Subsidiaries of investor-owned utilities were also very active overseas in 1994.

- It was announced that construction would not be completed on the last remaining active nuclear plant construction project in the United States.

- The interest in alternative energy sources for power generation continued to grow. Numerous announcements were made related to new wind, photovoltaic and geothermal projects. There were also several announcements for pilot fuel cell power plants.

- The deadline for Phase I of the Clean Air Act Amendments of 1990 occurred at the end of the year. All 110 power plants which were affected apparently were in compliance at the time the compliance deadline occurred.

- No definitive health hazards related to electric and magnetic field exposure have been confirmed, but 1994 saw at least three major EMF-related law suits against utilities. The cost of litigation and huge potential liability are making EMF a major concern for utilities.

1.3 Short Term Outlook

1995 will be another year of change and new direction for the industry. The four-year period of 1994, 1995, 1996 and 1997 will forever reshape the electric power industry in the United States. Six critical challenges for the electric power industry are:

- Customer access to transmission
- Independent power development
- Demand-side management
- Clean air restrictions
- Premature nuclear plant shutdown
- Gas contract risk management

Some important rulings and policy statements were made by the Federal Energy Regulatory Commission as well as state Public Utility Commissions in 1994. These will move into the marketplace in 1995.

According to Cambridge Energy Research Associates (Cambridge, MA), 1995 and 1996 could be a watershed period of potentially overwhelming change for the North

American electric power industry. In CERA's opinion, the changes expected to reshape the electric power industry include open access transmission, a second generation of independent power producers, a transformation of demand-side management (DSM) programs, air pollution restrictions, premature closure of nuclear power plants, and management of risks in long-term natural gas contracting. According to CERA, competitive forces vying to supply electricity in the future are likely to be brutal and less forgiving than the competition that arose out of the Public Utilities Regulatory Policies Act of 1978 (PURPA). However, the shape of the electric power industry in the future will be determined by how the above changes are carried out. Although the challenges facing the electric industry could seriously weaken regulated electric utilities, it is possible that the regulated industries could emerge as the winners. The regulated utilities could emerge leaner, tougher, and more in control of their own destinies than they have been since the 1970s.

1.4 Mid-Range and Long Term Outlook

As much as $30 trillion may be needed in energy infrastructure investments worldwide by 2020, according to the World Energy Council (Washington, DC). Driven by population increases and improved living conditions, global energy consumption demands will rise 130% to 200% of 1990 consumption by 2020.

According to RCG/Hagler Bailly, Inc., the remainder of the 1990s will be influenced by six market drivers:

• The future prevalence of utility integrated resource planning

- The demand for new power capacity

- The way the IP industry reacts to integrated resource planning

- The PUHCA reform and The Energy Policy Act of 1992

- The impacts of Order 636 and the availability of emission allowances

- The roles of key market facilitators such as fuel suppliers, financial organizations, turnkey contractors, and equipment suppliers

Over the next 20 years, electricity will capture an increasing share of the total energy market. According to a forecast by the U.S. Department of Energy, after growing from 24% in 1970 to 36% in 1990, the share of total primary energy consumed to produce electricity is expected to approach 39% by 2010. Stable electricity prices, effects of the Energy Policy Act of 1992, and continuing consumer preference for electricity cause growth in the demand for electricity to increase only slightly slower than economic growth. To meet this demand growth, between 149 GW and 245 GW of new generating capacity will be needed by 2010. As in recent years, nonutility generators are expected to provide a large share of the new capacity. Between 1990 and 2005, the majority of the new plants will be natural-gas-fired combined-cycle and turbine plants, added to serve intermediate and peak load requirements. After 2005, new coal-fired plants will be built to serve growing baseload needs.

Electrical World recently provided an electricity market forecast, "The Electric Power Industry 2010." Among the forecast's highlights were:

- Electricity markets are evolving toward a more competitive structure. This evolution has important implications for projected demand, power plant capacity additions and electricity price.

- Electric demand growth will average 2% through 2010. However, near-term growth will be significantly higher, based on comparisons with 1992's sluggish economy and mild summer.

- Electricity prices will remain stable on an inflation-adjusted basis through 2010, reflecting the lack of upward pressure from fixed costs or fuel prices.

The forecast predicts that while demand-side management activity on the part of utilities will increase five-fold by 2010, customers will respond to declining real energy prices over the foreseeable future by increasing their use of electricity. Such behavior is simply the flip side to customer-driven conservation which arose in response to high energy prices of the 1970s and early 1980s.

1.5 Opportunities

New markets and business activities have been opened by unique legislation related to the Energy Policy Act, including:

- New capacity marketing and brokering opportunities

- Opportunities for demand-side management (involving self-generation)

- New lines of business for regulated utilities and their affiliates involving transmission services

- An increased exploration of international markets for engineering, operations, construction, development and ownership purposes

- New forms of construction development using more build-own-transfer (BOT) techniques, and less traditional turnkey EPC contracting

- Post-PURPA management services after expiration of initial power agreements

- O&M services

- New requirements for international investment banking and project financing

2 DEREGULATION AND THE COMPETITIVE POWER MARKETPLACE

CONTENTS:

2.1 Trends and Market Assessment
2.2 Recent Activities
2.3 Short Term Outlook
2.4 Mid-Range and Long Term Outlook
2.5 Opportunities

2.1 Trends and Market Assessment

Deregulation effectively occurred as the federal government lifted restrictions on generating capacity of plants built by independent power producers. It has been accelerated by the Energy Policy Act of 1992, which requires utilities to wheel power produced by private wholesale generators.

In the wake of the Energy Policy Act, many observers have speculated on if and how utilities will adapt to a more competitive environment and how much of utilities' traditional activities will remain intact. Utilities are trying to develop novel approaches that will allow them to be competitive, shift risks, and earn returns that are not directly tied to asset growth. The emerging focus is vertical integration versus a narrowing of utility scope and concentrating on sustainable advantages. One manifestation of the new focus is for utilities to concentrate less on generating electricity and more on providing energy services by helping customers find ways to use electricity efficiently.

The most significant effect of the Energy Policy Act is that it changed the mindsets of the large utilities. Their search for ways to become more competitive will ultimately lead to a different kind of industry that is uniquely evolved for the United States. The principal driver will be least-cost power.

The Energy Policy Act of 1992 (EPA) created a new category of "exempt wholesale generators" (EWGs) under the Public Utility Holding Company Act of 1935 (PUHCA). The purpose of the new definition is to free EWGs from the requirements of PUHCA, which have proven to be a significant constraint on the development of competition in the wholesale power market. New Section 32 (a)(1) of PUHCA defines an EWG as any person determined by the FERC to be engaged directly, or indirectly through one or more affiliates, ... and exclusively in the business of owning or operating, or both owning and operating, all or part of one or more eligible facilities and selling electric energy at wholesale. Eligible facilities are defined as facilities that are used for the generation of electric energy exclusively for sale at wholesale, although retail sales are permitted for purely foreign facilities. Unlike a Qualifying Facility under PURPA, an EWG is not required to have a steam host, nor meet efficiency or operating standards. Domestic EWGs are regulated as public utilities, but may get many waivers if market-based rates are accepted. QFs are exempted from Federal Power Act regulation.

As of January 1994, the FERC had approved 67 of 90 EWG applications. More than half of the applications were made by utilities or utility affiliates.

According to the Edison Electric Institute, utilities are positioning themselves financially for the competitive world by:

- Reducing margins
- Reducing capacity margins
- Diversifying into IPPs, EWGs, and foreign facilities
- Lowering the capital intensity of generation
- Merging
- Instituting tailored service to customers

At the 1994 American Public Power Association (APPA) National Conference (Chicago), Royce Lyles (APPA President) and Larry Hobart (APPA Executive Director) provided some examples of how utilities are reassessing power supply relationships in response to new competition:

- The North American Electric Reliability Council is considering how to incorporate nonutility generators into its operations.

- State public utility commissions are increasingly relying on competitive bidding to obtain new power supplies.

- Contracts, as opposed to regulation, are becoming the vehicle of choice in determining prices.

- "Long-term" power supply agreements are measured in periods of 7 to 10 years today, down from the 25 to 30 years common in the 1970s.

- There is much more interest in buying power, as opposed to building it, and purchases are made in smaller amounts to more closely track load growth.

- Utilities are unbundling their electric supply components and selling them separately.

- Organizations have been set up to broker and market power.

The Dreiford Group points out that to envision a worst case deregulation scenario, utilities need only recall the painful lessons learned by the telecommunications spinoffs. They were late in grasping the wisdom of developing workable culture strategies in the same breath as effective competitive strategies. They discovered that poorly implemented downsizing could fail to produce increased profits and productivity gains, and poorly communicated ethics programs could fail in preventing lawsuits and financial penalties.

However, due to the higher cost of utility power generation plants and utility power purchase obligations under long-term contracts, many electric utilities do not want to transport this cheaper power to end-users since it would displace purchases of existing utility power resources. The Energy Policy Act of 1992 has increased the availability of transmission services for wholesale sellers and buyers of power, and FERC has been actively pursuing policies for increased access to such services, analogous to comparable changes in the gas industry.

Deregulation of the U.S. utility industry has wrought massive change in the engineering community. The whole nature of the business is changing. Utilities are downsizing, contracting out traditional services, and consolidating. Partnering is becoming commonplace. This compels consulting firms to accept new risk. Instead of being paid up front, firms are paid through revenues of some projects.

2.2 Recent Activities

What specific issues were of most concern to utility executives in 1994? Several surveys provided different views on how deregulation, competition and other challenges will affect the electric power industry.

A 1994 survey by Washington International Energy Group (Washington, DC) asked 285 senior U.S. utility executives to rank 23 issues on a scale of importance. Competition was ranked as the most important issue facing the utility industry today, with 76% of respondents choosing it as 'very important.' The other to issues were retail access (74%), open wholesale transmission access (70%), and improving revenue and earnings (65%). Nearly one-third of the executives who took part in the survey expect reliability of electric systems to decrease in the near future.

In response to competitive threats, most utilities have implemented measures to cut costs. Early retirement, layoffs, and consolidation are popular with many of the top U.S. companies. Most analysts believe that utilities are making the right move to streamline operations to stay competitive. An example cost reduction effort was the March 1994 severance plan of Duke Power Company, the nation's seventh largest investor-owned utility. Duke offered a generous separation package, ranging from six months pay for employees with three month's of service to $78,000 for a $52,000/year employee with 30 years experience. Previously, Duke had trimmed approximately 2,000 of its 19,500 employees.

Alexander & Alexander Services, Inc. has conducted an annual survey since 1987 of individuals in utility companies responsible for risk management and related financial decisions, asking them to rank, in order of importance to their companies, current U.S. legislative and regulatory issues. The 10 areas with the highest level of importance ranking in the 1994 survey are:

• Electromagnetic fields from high voltage transmissions lines and electric appliances
• Spiraling health care costs

- Caps on noneconomic and/or punitive damages

- Increased enforcement of environmental laws

- Continuation of soft property/casualty market (except tightening property exposure for windstorm and earthquake

- Court rulings on liability coverage for cleanups

- Modification of joint and several liability doctrine

- Self-insurance trends, including state regulation and identifying tax efficiencies

- Comprehensive legislation to restructure the Superfund statue

- Managed care programs

DoE Secretary Hazel O'Leary points out that all players have some stake in the future of the electric utility industry. At the 1994 Electricity Forum (Washington, DC), sponsored by the U.S. Department of Energy and the National Association of Regulatory Utility Commissioners, O'Leary identified the following perceived top concerns for the major groups of players:

- Utilities: stranded costs

- Consumers: low cost and equity

- Environmentalists: protection of demand-side management programs

- Federal Energy Regulatory Commission (FERC): security of the industry as a whole

- State regulators: lower costs

- Wall Street: return for risks

- Power producers: grid access

2.3 Short Term Outlook

There is a current shifting of priorities among electric utilities. In a survey of executives of investor-owned utilities, Future Technology Surveys, Inc. (Lilburn, GA) found that they foresee the ten top challenges they will face in 1997 are:

- Transmission access
- Environmental, pollution controls
- Deregulation
- Financial stability of utilities
- Competition from independent power producers
- Regulatory controls, rate controls
- Reliability
- Public image
- Human resources, training, productivity
- Reorganization and decentralization

This is a dramatic change from how executives ranked challenges in a 1992 survey of the same group:

- Regulatory controls, rate controls
- Environmental, pollution controls
- Reliability
- Financial stability of utilities
- Public image
- Reorganization and decentralization
- Fuel supplies and costs
- Transmission access
- Human resources, training, productivity
- Infrastructure, maintenance

2.4 Mid-Range and Long Term Outlook

Within the next several years, competition will focus on large, energy-intensive industrial and large commercial customers. Driven by the disparity in rates among neighboring and regional utilities, large users are expected to lobby aggressively for retail wheeling and access to new supplies.

New competitors will provide customers with additional supply options, forcing traditional utilities to offer better prices and or service. Competition at the point of end use will increase as the natural gas industry develops new end-use technologies, gas utilities will compete more aggressively, and some state regulatory commissions will promote fuel switching as part of integrated resource planning (IRP) and demand-side management (DSM). However, as long as electric utilities are subject to cost-based rate of return regulation within price-sensitive markets, they will be at a competitive disadvantage.

As a result, electric utilities are expected to unbundle their services into production (or generations), transmission (or wheeling), and distribution services to eliminate the cross subsidies inherent in current electric utility cost and rate structures as well as to compete more effectively. Electric utilities will not be unlike gas companies, which have vertically disaggregated and unbundled services since the mid-1980s. The costs of each unbundled service will have significant implications for the overall and niche competitiveness of individual electric utilities.

According to The Dreiford Group, if utilities are to weather the gathering storm deregulation is bringing, they must hasten to balance a strategy for the present with a strategy for the future. Through 2000 and 2005, retail wheeling may create full-scale open competition for customers among local utilities everywhere. With California, Michigan and New Mexico leading the way, U.S. consumers in every state will benefit from weekend electricity rates and service options if they choose to shop for them. The

Dreilinger Group recommends the following game plan for utilities to cope with the challenges of deregulation:

- Develop/promote new customer oriented vision
- Demonstrate personal support for new goals
- Provide necessary resources
- Mobilize and energize supporters for changes
- Stress goals and ends rather than means
- Orchestrate and champion a continuous learning environment

2.5 Opportunities

Deregulation and competition have given rise to a new players in the U.S. power market -- the power marketer and power broker. Power brokers are already springing up across the United States. In an effort to capture the benefits of the new competitive market, numerous companies, including affiliates of established energy industry companies, have filed rate schedules and sought regulatory waivers and approvals to market and for broker electricity. In the electric industry, power is available for sale from large, capacity-rich utilities, as well as from various independent power producers. Much of this power may be priced below the power purchase and generation costs bundled into utilities' sales rates. Large industrial end-users would like to buy this cheap power to reduce their manufacturing costs and increase their competitiveness.

According to *Electric Utility Week*, power marketers, starting what they see as a revolution of sorts in electricity markets, are bringing derivatives to electricity, allowing buyers and sellers to minimize their exposure to changes in power costs. At least two power marketers, Citizens Power & Light and Enron Power Marketing, are negotiating deals in which they limit the effect of changes in electricity prices on their customers and link the customer's buy or sell price to the price of another commodity. The New York Mercantile Exchange plans to begin trading in electricity futures contracts.

It appears that power marketers will wield a significant degree of control in the industry, and it will be essential for IPPs to work with APMs as exchange agents for their product.

In 1994, FERC issued a ruling which permits affiliated power marketers (APMs) to charge market-based rates provided that they meet certain conditions. FERC is still defining what constitutes classification as an affiliated power marketer, but it basically is any group with more than 5% or 10% ownership by an electric utility, QF or IPP. Until a formal policy, FERC is reviewing all power sales by APMs on a case-by-case basis.

The Power Marketing Association was formed in October 1994. The Alexandria, VA-based organization will support the power marketer with publications, conferences, seminars, studies, testimony and surveys.

3 INVESTOR-OWNED ELECTRIC UTILITIES

CONTENTS:

3.1 Trends and Market Assessment
3.2 Recent Activities
3.3 Short Term Outlook
3.4 Mid-Range and Long Term Outlook
3.5 Opportunities

3.1 Trends and Market Assessment

In June 1994, *Electric Light & Power* ranked the top 100 investor-owned electric utilities. The top 10 in revenue, based on 1993 financial performances are:

- Pacific Gas & Electric Company
- Southern Company
- SCEcorp
- Consolidated Edison
- Public Service Enterprise Group
- Texas Utilities
- Florida Power & Light Company
- American Electric Power
- Commonwealth Edison
- Entergy

The electric utility industry is currently undergoing a fundamental transition. As a growing, capital-intensive industry, utilities historically placed heavy emphasis on the production side of the business. Over the years, this allowed the electric utility industry to gain significant experience with the supply side of the business. The risks associated with actions on the supply side were generally known, and due to the high growth occurring in the boom years of the industry, precise evaluation of the performance of marketing programs was not that critical. Moreover, the relative value added by marketing programs was limited compared to the growth contributed by the expanding economy.

Currently, the electric utility industry seems to be moving into a new frontier. For some electric utilities, the greatest value added for electric service may come from the demand-side of the business. It does not matter whether a utility's load shape objective is strategic load growth or conservation, future customer benefits may result largely from how well a utility is able to market to its customers. This turnabout stems largely from the fact that the electric utility industry has matured. Uncontrolled growth in the future may lead to poor financial performance and perhaps higher rates.

Integrated resource planning (IRP) has changed the way utilities plan for the future. The National Association of Regulatory Utility Commissioners (NARUC) defines IRP as "a way of analyzing growth and operation of utilities that considers a wide variety of both supply and demand factors so the optimal way of providing electric service to the public can be determined." A November 1993 report by the Edison Electric Institute found the following status of state IRP programs:

- Adopted and implemented: 13 states
- Partially adopted and implemented: 18 states
- First steps taken: 7 states
- Not done much so far: 12 states

A 1994 study by DynCorp-Meridian for the National Renewable Energy Laboratory found that 30 of 51 jurisdictions studies (e.g., 50 states plus the District of Columbia) had integrated resource planning statutes.

3.2 Recent Activities

The issue of stranded investment has emerged as the focal point of the impact of the evolving competition in the U.S. electric power industry. At risk to investor-owned utilities are $200 billion or more in generating facilities which may become 'stranded' (i.e., obsolete or unnecessary) when utility customers stop buying power from the utility and, instead, purchase transmission services from that utility to get power purchased from someone else.

In June 1994, the Federal Energy Regulatory Commission issued a proposed rulemaking which would serve as a framework for dealing with recovery of stranded investments. States will have the first opportunity to deal with stranded cost issues within their jurisdictions, and FERC urged states to promptly deal with the issue. For states that fail to do so, FERC proposed its framework for approaching the recovery of utility investments. FERC distinguished between wholesale and retail stranded costs.

Wholesale stranded costs, which occur when the utility was selling electricity for later resale and the customer stopped buying, will be dealt with by FERC with primary importance being given to the contract. For contracts which existed prior to the time of the rulemaking, utilities could seek recovery of such costs only if their contracts contained explicit stranded cost provisions. Existing contracts which do not contain such provisions may be renegotiated during a three-year transitional period. The utility could seek recovery of stranded investment through transmission rates during the transition period. For new contracts, a utility would not be allowed to recover stranded costs through transmission rates.

Retail stranded costs, which occur when a utility's retail customer begins to purchase only transmission service from the utility, should be dealt with by the states. If states do not explicitly address the issue, FERC may consider requests to recover stranded retail costs. Retail stranded costs will represent the larger case, since only 10% to 15% of generating investment by investor-owned utilities is in the wholesale rate base.

The Electric Generation Association (EGA), the trade association for independent power generators, outlined its position on stranded investment in late-1994. EGA stated that electric utilities should be able to recover lost costs stranded by the transition to competition, and supported the principle of honoring existing power purchase agreements. EGA feels that the extent of the recovery should depend upon the terms for which the parties had bargained.

FERC's specific positions on stranded investment also began to take shape in 1994. The Commission established that the recovery of stranded investment recovery is not automatic in every situation when it rejected the recovery of stranded investment charges as part of transmission service rates in a major case involving AEP in early 1994. In the Blue Ridge case, AEP was unable to support its claim that it reasonably expected Virginia Municipals to continue to take service from Appalachian beyond the 40 MW involved in the case (representing less than 0.167% of AEP's generating capacity), and was directed to delete a stranded investment charge from its revised service.

A federal appellate court decision in 1994 overturned the Federal Energy Regulatory Commission's 1992 decision to allow Entergy to recover legitimate and verifiable stranded investment costs. Although the case can be read as rejecting the concept of recovery for such costs, several Commissions have said the agency's recently announced stranded investment rulemaking will satisfy the concerns of the court. The Entergy case, resulting from a 1991 FERC filing, was the first to pose the question of how utilities might recover the costs of their investment in generating facilities that become stranded when customers leave the utility.

In resolving the issue of stranded costs, Northeast Utilities and one of its customers agreed to pay Central Maine Power Company $10 million in compensation for the customer's decision to drop Central Maine as a power supplier. The parties involved said the settlement was one of the first that addresses how, and to what degree, power suppliers will be able to recoup the high cost of their investments when they lose business under new federal regulations that allow utilities to vie for each other's business. The settlement, subject to regulatory clearance, cleared the way for Madison Electric Works (Madison, ME), a municipally owned utility, to buy power from Northeast Utilities (Hartford, CT) at prices below those previously charged by Central Maine (Augusta, ME).

3.3 Short Term Outlook

Not all investor-owned utilities are being affected equally in the new competitive environment, and some well positioned utilities may benefit in 1995. The impact will depend on several factors, including the cost of producing and transmitting electricity, sales and customer mix, reserve margins, geography, and state and federal regulation. One thing already is certain, being a low-cost producer of electricity will be crucial to maintaining market share and sustaining credit quality. Conversely, high-cost producers with substantial wholesale or energy-intensive industrial or large commercial loads, particularly in regions with large amounts of reserve capacity, are most vulnerable.

The most likely scenario evolving in 1995 of the impact of competition in the U.S. electric utility industry is that the strongest companies willhold their own and retain a healthy return-on-investment, the weakest companies will fail, and the industry as a whole declines in profitability. This scenario was first presented by Mitch Diamond at an EEI Financial Conference.

One of the challenges of 1995 for most utilities will be operating with a smaller organization than they had one or two years ago. Downsizing has been prevalent among utilities. Pacific Gas & Electric Company began the trend in 1993, announcing the near elimination of its 4,750-member engineering and construction staff. American Electric Power cut about 1,040 positions as part of its restructuring program. Wisconsin Electric Power Company will cut its in-house engineering staff in half. One of the major engineering firms reports about one public utility inquiry a month associated with outsourcing brought on by cutbacks.

3.4 Mid-Range and Long Term Outlook

A recent survey by R.J. Rudden Associates, Inc. (Hauppauge, NY) and Fitch Investors Service, Inc. made a comprehensive assessment of state regulatory policies as they concern the effects which increased competition will bring to bear on electric utilities. The current status and timing of implementation of competitive practices within the 33 states are:

- Retail wheeling by industrial and/or large commercial customers is currently implemented in only one state, but is expected to experience rapid growth between 1995 and 2000, and beyond.

- Self-generation, municipalization and fuel substitution are permitted within 20, 18 and 17 states, respectively.

- Six commissions require wholesale wheeling within their jurisdictions and seven commissions prohibit retail wheeling within their jurisdictions.

The highlights of the survey are:

- 90% of commissions believe business risk will escalate

- 87% project an increased need for unbundled and market-flexible electric rates

- 82% feel utilities will face higher cost of capital

- 70% see a risk of utilities not earning their authorized rate of return

- 38% expect investor-owned electric utility bankruptcies in their jurisdictions

Thirty-three state regulatory commissions participated in the survey. The following list represents business risks and regulatory practices 50% or more respondents felt would increase as a result of competition within the electric utility industry. The percent of respondents expecting an increase is indicated next to each issue.

- Overall business risk of electric utilities (90.3%)
- Need for market-flexible rates (87.1%)
- Need for unbundled rates (87.1%)
- Cost of capital (81.5%)
- Level of regulatory vigilance required (77.4%)
- Rate of utility industry vertical disaggregation (76.7%)
- Risk of not earning authorized rates of return (70.4%)
- Need for electric integrated resource planning (IRP) (62.5%)
- Rate of mergers and acquisitions (62.1%)
- Rate at which utilities will horizontally aggregate (58.6%)
- Need for regional electric IRP (56.7%)
- Rates to captive customers (55.2%)
- Speed with which electric investor-owned utilities (IOUs) will downsize (54.8%)
- Level of customer complaints (51.7%)
- Need for prudence reviews (51.6%)

Remarkably, 38% of the respondents felt that electric IOU bankruptcies, within their jurisdictions, would increase as a result of the combined effects of the six forms of competition, with the major threats coming from retail wheeling and self-generation.

The factors that respondents feel would most enhance an electric utility company's market position are:

- Electric integrated resource planning and demand-side management
- Deployment of new electric end-use technologies
- Use of unbundled, marginal cost-based, and incentive rates
- Downsizing

In assessing the implications of the results of the R.J. Rudden survey, Roger Feldman of McDermott, Will & Emery (Washington, DC) observed in *The Cogeneration Monthly Letter* (November 1994) the following:

- There are going to be a lot of generating assets available in the market, probably marked down, and likely competing with IPP power.

- There is going to be an evaluation of the merits of purchased power strategies in a new setting: bankruptcy (or ratemaking for firms close to it).

- There are going to be consolidations which trigger reexamination of the power sources to be considered for dispatch.

- There may be a shrinkage of potential industrial customers.

3.5 Opportunities

The downsizing of investor-owned electric utilities will create opportunities in systems integration/outsourcing. As electric utilities downsize and reduce engineering departments, they are contracting out for more engineering services. An increasing number of electric utilities are diversifying in an effort to combat skyrocketing expenses and shrinking rate bases, according to a prediction made by senior utility industry consultants at Cresap, the general management consulting firm of Towers Perrin. According to Frost & Sullivan (Mountain View, CA), the systems integration/outsourcing market will (all industry, not utilities only) grow from $32 billion in 1992 to $104 billion in 1999, an 18.5% average annual growth rate.

According to *Nonutility Business Activities of Investor-Owned Utilities*, published in 1994 by the Edison Electric institute, utilities are entering into market outside of their core utility business at a much faster pace than they did in 1994. Most utilities have experienced substantial increases in revenues from diversified ventures, reaching more than $5.8 billion. The EEI study found that 74 of 99 utilities had nonutility businesses that comprised at least 1% of total corporate assets. The most frequent ventures being entered into are:

- IPP, cogeneration and alternative energy
- Real estate
- International

- Engineering services and products
- Leasing, factoring, credit
- Passive investments
- Gas transmission, storage
- Oil/gas exploration, development, marketing
- Mining
- Communications
- Venture capital
- Environmental

Utility Data Institute, Inc. studied more than 2,000 diversified utility firms, and found the majority are involved in areas familiar to utilities, such as electric power generation, oil and gas extraction, mining, finance, and real estate. A distribution of utility diversification by business area is:

- Retailing and services: 21%
- Mining; oil and gas: 20%
- Financial: 20%
- Transportation: 12%
- Real estate: 10%
- Manufacturing: 7%
- Cogeneration, independent power production: 6%
- Other: 4%

According to Future Technology Surveys (Lilburn, GA), 3% of electric utility income, including that of subsidiaries, was from diversification into activities other than power generation in 1992. This is forecast to increase to 10% in 1997 and remain at 10% until 2002.

Some utilities are finding innovative opportunities for cost reduction. Long Island Lighting Company has developed a very unique approach to cost reduction. More than 500,000 old timber utility poles will be wrapped in fiberglass sheets, extending their 30-year life by 15 years. The savings will be $2,000 per pole, or $1 billion.

4 INDEPENDENT POWER

CONTENTS:

4.1 Trends and Market Assessment
4.2 Recent Activities
4.3 Short Term Outlook
4.4 Mid-Range and Long Term Outlook
4.5 Opportunities

4.1 Trends and Market Assessment

According to the Electric Generation Association (Washington, DC), since 1990,

IPPs have accounted for 50% or more of new electric generation capacity completed in

the United States.

According to information presented at the 1994 Competitive Power Congress

(Philadelphia), the top ten independent power firms and their capacity are:

- Exxon Energy: 5,659 MW
- Mission Energy: 2,741 MW
- National Power International: 2,612 MW
- Enron Power: 2,039 MW
- PowerGen: 1,977 MW
- Sithe Energies: 1,761 MW
- AES: 1,663 MW
- Hopewell Holdings: 1,450 MW
- Destec Energy: 1,291 MW
- British Gas: 1,231 MW

To reach positions of advantage quickly, many players in the U.S. power industry (non-utility developers, utility affiliates, equipment suppliers, and engineering and construction firms), are seeking to form alliances with other key players in the industry, both for the U.S. market and for overseas ventures. These alliances take various forms, such as formal partnerships, joint ventures, or less structured mutual agreements to join forces, either for a single specific project or in a longer-term arrangement. U.S. Generating Company (Bethesda, MD) is one of the best-known industry alliance. It is a long-term joint venture between units of construction giant Bechtel Corporation and investor-owned utility Pacific Gas & Electric, both of San Francisco. Other examples include alliances formed between NRG Energy, a development subsidiary of Northern States Power Company (Minneapolis, MN) and PowerGen plc (London); U.S. developer AES Corporation (Arlington, VA), with a unit of Tractebel, the national utility of Belgium; and equipment supplier U.S. Turbine with Japanese equipment firms Mitsubishi and Kawasaki.

4.2 Recent Activities

RCG/Hagler Bailly, Inc. (Arlington, VA) has published an annual profile of the U.S. independent power market since 1986. Highlights of the 1994 publication are:

- In 1993, 66 projects came on-line, adding 2,856 MW.

- 23,500 MW of new projects were announced in 1993.

- Capacity under development declined in 1993 from 93 GW to 74 GW.

- Natural gas is the primary energy source accounting for 64 GW or 51% of active capacity.

- The five top states (Washington, New York, California, New Jersey, and Florida) account for 29 GW or 39% of capacity under development.

- Major growth in capacity under development occurred in the Pacific Northwest and the Mountain Region.

- IPPs/EWGs account for 25% or 31 GW of active capacity, down from 28% and 39.5 GW in the previous year.

- The shift to larger projects continues; average size of projects announced in 1993 was 138 MW.

According to *Independent Energy*, the highlights of 1994 for the independent

power business were:

- Nearly $20 billion in financial activity during the past year. Up from approximately $11 billion in 1993. Project finance is nearly $9.5 billion.

- More than 6,000 MW of capacity were expected to come on-line during the past 12 months.

- International markets continued to expand, creating more opportunities for project development. A cap on the rate of return in China slowed progress there, while India's market opened considerably.

- California's Public Utilities Commission issues its *Blue Book*, which if implemented, would restructure the state's electrical generation, transmission and distribution system and give consumers freedom to choose their supplier.

- Successful trade missions are conducted by the U.S. Department of Energy and U.S. Department of Commerce. The DoE mission to India leds to 11 potential deals being signed by U.S. power generation companies and several contracts.

- New sources of funding projects were developed, including rated debt securities, Eurobonds, 114A capital, investment funds and private placements. Developers looked more to export credit agencies and multilateral lenders.

According to the Electric Generation Association (Washington, DC), the Federal

Energy Regulatory Commission received 38 Exempt Wholesale Generator applications during the first six months of FY1994. The trend is clearly for independent power producers to apply for EWG status rather than taking the Qualifying Facility route. In FY1993, FERC received 80 EWG applications and approved 65. Virtually all of the EWG applications are coming from independents, even though utilities have the opportunity to reclassify existing power plants as EWGs.

A power marketing agency is emerging in the Pacific Northwest that intends to match utilities and manufacturing firms who want power with private producers. The new agency, Power Resource Managers Inc., an offshoot of CH2M Hill Inc., has lined up a dozen utilities and five aluminum companies as interested customers in competing with the Bonneville Power Administration. Independent power producers involved are J. Makowski Company (Seattle, WA), ARK Energy (Laguna Hills, CA) and Coburg Power (Portland, OR).

In July 1994, Pacific Gas & Electric Company and Bechtel Group, Inc. announced their partnership in independent power production, U.S. Generating Company, had reached an agreement for the acquisition of J. Makowski Company, Inc. JMC is involved in the development of natural gas-fueled power generation, natural gas distribution, supply, and underground storage projects, and was valued in the range of $250 million to $300 million.

4.3 Short Term Outlook

While IPPs are increasing their activities internationally, they are experiencing a slacking in U.S. demand growth. According RCG/Hagler Bailly, Inc., IPPs now have

74,000 MW under development in the United States, down from 93,000 MW a year ago.

Some of the reasons that U.S. independent power developers are moving in favor of international opportunities, was discussed by Charles Goff, President of Destec Energy (Dallas, TX), in a presentation at Power-Gen (Dallas, TX). Other nations are making their power markets more attractive to outside investors and developers, while IPPs are experiencing risk here. According to Goff, utilities contribute to U.S. IPP problems, because some are not sincere in their RFP (request-for-proposal) process and their contracts for purchased power. In many cases, utilities operate bidding programs that require independents to incur large expenses up front to make proposals, then the utilities decide to build new capacity themselves and not from IPPs. Utilities cancelled for deferred 6 GW worth of RFPs in the first half of 1993. Aggravating the problem is a new policy from the federal Rural Electrification Administration requiring all co-op borrowers to conduct an IPP bidding program before building any new capacity. Most have gone through the motions of accepting bids and then decided to go forward with their own plant construction. So far, 12 co-ops have conducted such programs but only one, Oglethorpe Electric Cooperative in Georgia, has committed to a third-party for new capacity. Utility regulatory commissions are also second-guessing IPP contracts and tinkering with economics after the fact, according to Goff; regulators in several states are "ignoring the sanctity of previously negotiated power contracts and want to rebid the deal or, in some cases, even cancel projects after the independent developer has spent millions of dollars in a good-faith effort to bring the project into operation."

There are still strong opportunities for IPPs domestically. These were discussed by John Siegel, Vice President of Bechtel Power Corporation at the same Power Gen meeting. He predicted a strong role for IPPs in the U.S. power market through 2004. Siegel expects utilities and non-utilities to share equally in a market for 140 GW of new orders and about 100 GW of new, installed capacity. Non-utility generators comprise 73% of the commitments announced in 1992 for new baseload capacity. Those commitments were for 33 new generating projects, totaling 6.5 GW.

4.4 Mid-Range and Long Term Outlook

According RCG/Hagler Bailly, Inc., between 40 GW and 56 GW of new independent power capacity will come on-line by 2004.

According to A.T. Donnelly of Barakat & Chamberlin, Inc. (Portland, OR), the Pacific Northwest continues on the cutting edge of advancement of the nation's independent power industry. The region's growing energy deficit and the move by Bonneville Power Administration's (BPA's) customers to find alternative sources of power are only a few of the drivers for change in the electricity business. Other drivers of change in the pacific northwest electricity marketplace are:

- Energy deficit is not 550 MW.
- Capacity deficit will occur by 1999.
- BPA is restructuring, proposing two-tiered rate structure.
- U.S. Ninth Circuit Court decisions require increased use of Columbia River system for salmon run recovery.
- U.S. Supreme Court rulings now give states more authority over permitting of dams.

- The 1992 Energy Policy Act has fostered two new Regional Transmission Groups (RTGs) in the Northwest.

- Retail wheeling appears inevitable, beginning in California within several years.

4.5 Opportunities

Trends such as utility-sponsored cogeneration, and repowering of aging utility generating plants could significantly restrict future opportunities for independents who have focused exclusively on wholesale generation, at least in the United States. Independents face a different, more sophisticated marketplace that now seeks the best energy value, rather than simply looking for sources of power supply. If independents want to maintain a healthy bottom line, they will need to look for strategic advantages. Sam Barakat, Barakat & Chamberlin, offers four ways in which independents might obtain such a strategic advantage:

- Seek to become dominant in a particular technology, such as geothermal, hydroelectricity, or coal gasification.

- Achieve a recognized position of market leadership; such as Mission Energy, with its development of many plants both domestically and internationally.

- Attempt to assure reliable long-term access to important resources needed for successful development, such as natural gas transmission.

- Strive to manage their development process very carefully, with strict controls on overhead and other costs.

Wheeling presents an opportunity for producers of cogenerated power. Cogeneration facilities are sited at the thermal host, and the purchaser of electricity is usually co-located. Electricity is sold to the interconnected electric utility and/or to the thermal host. If power can be wheeled to a different party, additional opportunities appear with the removal of the co-location constraint. Other customers can sometimes be located that will pay more for electricity. According to ERC, Inc., the best market opportunities for cogenerated power are as follows:

- Non-interconnected utilities with high avoided costs

- Requirements utilities

- Industrial plants within a requirement utility's service territory

- Retail affiliate of a non-utility generator (NUG) or exempt wholesale generator (EWG)

- Mutually beneficial situations

5 THE ELECTRIC POWER MARKET

CONTENTS:

5.1 Trends and Market Assessment
5.2 Recent Activities
5.3 Short Term Outlook
5.4 Mid-Range and Long Term Outlook
5.5 Opportunities

5.1 Trends and Market Assessment

Historically, growth in the demand for electricity has been closely tied to economic growth. Until the 1970s and 1980s, growth in electricity demand tended to outpace economic growth. However, the rapid rise in energy prices in the 1970s and early 1980s, combined with growing market saturation of electric appliances, dampened this relationship -- narrowing it to nearly one-to-one by the late 1980s. According to the Energy Information Administration, this trend is expected to continue, with electricity demand actually growing more slowly than the economy over the next two decades.

5.2 Recent Activities

In 1994, statistics for electric power demand and sales were tabulated and published for the preceding year by the Energy Information Administration of the U.S.

Department of Energy and Edison Electric Institute.

According to the Energy Information Administration, electricity sales in 1993 were 2.9 trillion kWH, 3.7% above 1992 sales. The 1992 to 1993 increase was the largest year to year increase since 1988. Sales in the commercial sector rose 3.8% and electricity sales to the industrial sector rose 1.0%.

According to Edison Electric Institute, retail sales revenues to U.S. electric utilities was $186.7 billion in 1993. Retail sales were 2,730 GWh, and summer peak demand was 548,700 MW.

According to a preliminary analysis by the Energy Information Administration, the 1994 U.S. electric demand and supply market was characterized as follows:

- Electricity demand growth continued to rise in 1994 at a rate of 3.3%, close to the 1993 rate.

- Growth in residential demand for electricity in 1994 was 2.8%. Growth in commercial sector demand was 5.5% in 1994.

- Industrial demand growth in 1994 was 2.3%.

- Oil and natural gas generation experienced the greatest expansion in 1994, while hydropower decreased. Lower prices for oil and gas prompt rising utility use of these fuels, and below normal water conditions in the West, particularly in the Northwest, restrict hydropower.

- Net imports of electricity from Canada were high in 1994. This is due mainly to increased interruptible purchases from Ontario Hydro and Hydro Quebec, which have been pursuing markets for their surplus electricity. They have good water conditions and offer competitive prices compared to other available electricity in the surrounding areas.

- Coal generation in 1994 did not grow as rapidly as in 1993 due to compliance with the Clean Air Act. In 1994, nuclear generation grew by 2.5% because of projected increases in capacity and efficiency.

- U.S. utilities generated about 2.1% more electricity in 1994. Non-utility generation increased at an even faster rate of 9.0% in 1994, as a result of capacity additions.

In early 1994, New York Power Authority cancelled a $5 billion, 20-year power contract with Hydro-Quebec. The reasons cited were budget cuts, environmental factors, higher nuclear plant expectations, a decline in projected fuel prices since 1989 when the original contract was negotiated, and about 4-million kilowatts of non-utility generating capacity in New York beyond what was anticipated.

5.3 Short Term Outlook

The Energy Information Administration provides the following outlook for the 1995 U.S. electric demand and supply market:

- In 1995, the slowing economy and assumed normal weather results in somewhat lower growth in electricity demand than in 1994.

- Growth in commercial demand for electricity is projected at 2.9% in 1995, due primarily to expanding employment.

- In 1995, industrial demand growth is projected to rise by 1.9%, reflecting the increases in manufacturing production.

- Net imports of electricity from Canada are not expected to be as high in 1995 as in 1994. The surplus electricity may be needed to meet internal Canadian demand.

- Growth in coal generation in 1995 is not expected, due to compliance with the Clean Air Act. No further increases in nuclear capacity are expected for 1995.

- U.S. utilities are expected to generate approximately 1.2% more electricity in 1995. Nonutility generation is expected to increase 6.6% in 1995, as a result of capacity additions.

The average age of power plants in the United States will exceed 26 years in 1995, which is almost their expected life. Life extension programs to maintain reliability are unproven, but repowering will be necessary to avoid the entire fleet of plants from becoming obsolete at once. Using EPRI's data regarding power plant additions and subtractions, it is estimated that there will be 100,000 MW on the plus side and 150,000 MW on the negative side between now and 2000. Therefore, without any growth in electricity demand, there will be a loss of 50,000 MW in capacity by the turn of the century.

American utilities currently have a surplus of electric power capacity. However, with demand forecast to grow 2.2% annually, regions of this county will soon be starving for additional generating capacity attributed to the lack of new orders. This shortage could easily become critical in the late-1990s.

5.4 Mid-Range and Long Term Outlook

In the *Annual Energy Outlook 1994*, the Energy Information Administration of the U.S. Department of Energy published three forecast scenarios for energy prices, supply, demand, and imports over the next two decades. The three cases are based on existing legislation, including the Energy Policy Act of 1992 and regulations, without incorporating any proposed legislation, or regulations. The purpose of the Reference Case is to facilitate comparisons among the other cases; it should not be viewed as the most likely scenario. The Reference Case combines the assumption of an annual economic growth rate of 2%; the High Economic Growth Case makes an assumption of higher macroeconomic growth (2.4% per year); and the Low Economic Growth Case assumes lower macroeconomic growth (1.6% per year). All three assume a mid-level path for the world oil price.

For the three cases, electricity sales are as follows (for reference, 1992 sales were 2763 billion kWh):

- 2000
  Reference case: 3,112 billion kWh
  High economic growth case: 3,178 billion kWh
  Low economic growth case: 3,046 billion kWh

- 2010 (annual growth 1992-2101 in parenthesis)
  Reference case: 3,469 billion kWh (1.3%)
  High economic growth case: 3,631 billion kWh (1.5%)
  Low economic growth case: 3,307 billion kWh (1.0%)

For the Reference Case, electricity sales by sector are forecast as follows (1992 data provided for reference):

- 1992
  Residential: 936 billion kWh
  Commercial: 850 billion kWh
  Industrial: 973 billion kWh
  Transportation: 4 billion kWh
  Total: 2,763 billion kWh

- 2000
  Residential: 995 billion kWh
  Commercial: 967 billion kWh
  Industrial: 1,126 billion kWh
  Transportation: 39 billion kWh
  Total: 3,296 billion kWh

- 2010 (annual growth 1992-2101 in parenthesis)
  Residential: 1,065 billion kWh (0.7%)
  Commercial: 1,030 billion kWh (1.1%)
  Industrial: 1,318 billion kWh (1.7%)
  Transportation: 56 billion kWh (15.8%)

Total: 3,469 billion kWh (1.3%)

For the Reference Case, generation by group is forecast as follows (1992 data provided for reference):

- 1992
  Electric utilities: 2,798 billion kWh
  Non-utility generators: 60 billion kWh
  Cogeneration: 192 billion kWh
  Net imports: 28 billion kWh

- 2000
  Electric utilities: 3,072 billion kWh
  Non-utility generators: 151 billion kWh
  Cogeneration: 210 billion kWh
  Net imports: 26 billion kWh

- 2010 (annual growth 1992-2101 in parenthesis)
  Electric utilities: 3,260 billion kWh (0.9%)
  Non-utility generators: 338 billion kWh (10.1%)
  Cogeneration: 235 billion kWh (1.1%)
  Net imports: 30 billion kWh (0.4%)

Through 2000 and beyond, electricity's role in U.S. energy markets will continue to grow. Relatively stable prices and the consumers' desire for convenient, versatile electric appliances combine to stimulate increased consumption of electricity. End-use efficiency improvements dampen growth in energy consumption, but, even so, growth in the demand for electricity lags only slightly behind economic growth.

Electricity will garner a growing share of total energy consumption; however, price-induced conservation, legislative action, and utility investments in demand-side management programs are expected to increase efficiency in end-use electricity markets, slowing growth. For instance, the Energy Policy Act of 1992 encourages utilities to use least-cost planning, a process that couples demand-side options directly with supply-side resource options and should slow growth in demand. Nonetheless, economic growth and growth in demand for electricity are expected to parallel one another. Between 1995 and 2010, the increase in demand for electricity will range from 1.0% to 1.5% each year, which is slightly slower than economic growth. This growth in electric demand will result from:

- Stable prices: Compared with the prices of other energy sources, the price of electricity is projected to increase at a lower rate.

- End-use convenience and versatility: At the point of end-use (home, office, and factory), electricity has a wide array of uses. Consumer desire for convenient electric appliances, such as air conditioners, facsimile machines, and computers, is expected to stimulate growth in the demand for electricity and partially offset the effect of improved end-use energy efficiency.

- Local environmental benefits: While power plants have considerable environmental impacts, the consumption of electricity in appliances and industrial processes produces virtually no harmful emissions.

Within the end-use sectors, the demand for electricity will increase more robustly in the commercial and industrial sectors than in the residential sector. A projected population growth rate of less than 1% per year restrains growth in residential energy demand, however stronger economic growth, when combined with the continued penetration of electricity-using technologies and processes, particularly in the industrial sector, will lead to more rapid consumption of electricity in the commercial and industrial sectors.

5.5 Opportunities

The biggest changes will occur in the residential sector. According to *Electric Utilities: Challenges to 2004*, published by Parks Associates (Dallas, TX), consumer demand for electricity usage will grow at a pace faster than most analysts' expectations. With new residential energy management technologies implemented over interactive networks, utilities will be able to manage energy load for residential customers.

6 WHOLESALE WHEELING

CONTENTS:

6.1 Trends and Market Assessment
6.2 Recent Activities
6.3 Short Term Outlook
6.4 Mid-Range and Long Term Outlook
6.5 Opportunities

6.1 Trends and Market Assessment

According to ERC, Inc., prior the Energy Policy Act of 1992, the economically viable market for wholesale wheeling was about 25,000 MW . Passage of the EPAct increased the total wholesale wheeling market to over 110,000 MW.

The EPAct states that a "person generating electric energy for resale may apply to the Commission" (FERC) "for an order...requiring a transmitting utility to provide transmission services." The order must meet the requirements of Section 212 and "be in the public interest." This latter condition will not be difficult to meet.

Power pools, a primary vehicle for wholesale wheeling, are growing in importance in the new era of competitive power. A power pool is a formal or informal agreement among a group of utilities to establish principles and criteria to coordinate the planning and/or operation of their bulk power facilities. Agreements establishing formal pools must be approved by the FERC. For example, the New York Power Pool (NYPP) coordinates virtually all of New York's energy demand through its seven investor-owned utility members and the Power Authority of the State of New York. NYPP's operations control center near Albany monitors the status of over 10,000 miles of transmission lines throughout the state, as well as conditions in the neighboring New England Power Pool; the Pennsylvania, New Jersey, Maryland Interconnection; the Maritime Pool (New Brunswick and Nova Scotia); Hydro-Quebec, and Ontario Hydro. The major U.S. power pools are:

- Central Area Power Coordination Group (CAPCO)
- Connecticut Valley Electric Exchange (CONVEX)
- Florida Electric Coordinated System
- Michigan Electric Coordinated Systems
- Mid-Continent Area Power Pool (MAPP)
- Missouri Basin Systems Group, Inc. (MBSG)
- MOKAN (Missouri-Kansas) Pool
- New England Power Pool (NEPOOL)
- New Mexico Power Pool
- New York Power Pool (NYPP)
- Northwest Power Pool Coordinating Group
- Pennsylvania-New Jersey-Maryland Interconnection (PJM)
- Rhode Island-Eastern Massachusetts-Vermont Energy Control (REMVEC)
- Southern California Utility Power Pool
- Wisconsin Power Pool

The proper pricing of transmission services is essential to efficient operation of the grid. Wheeling rights have little meaning if capacity on existing lines is scarce and there is no incentive to build new lines. Depending on the type of transmission pricing policies FERC adopts, the Commission may be able to encourage more voluntary wheeling service, and influence decisions to build or upgrade the supply of facilities.

While approximately 1,350 transmission rate schedules were filed at FERC through 1984, there have been relatively few cases in which the level or design of wheeling rates have been an issue in a contested proceeding (since most have been mutually agreed to by the parties). However, even though transmission rate matters have not been the subject of extensive litigation or rulemakings, the Commission has established more or less definitive policies with respect to several pricing issues, including:

- The use of embedded cost rates

- The use of average transmission operating and maintenance costs and average transmission losses

- Limitations on "percentage adders" in purchase/resale transactions and wheeling of interchange and fuel conservation energy transactions

6.2 Recent Activities

The Federal Energy Regulatory Commission is using its power to force high-voltage transmission system owners to provide access to their systems for other electricity buyers and sellers, as allowed by the Energy Policy Act. Initially, FERC influenced transmission access by requiring provision for more open access as part of several proposed utility mergers. In early 1994, FERC ordered Florida Power & Light Company to provide network access to Florida Municipal Power Agency. FERC ruled that since FMPA wants to be able to use the transmission system exactly as freely as Florida Power and Light does, it must pay a rate that reflects that equality. It must share the costs of the system on the same basis as Florida Power & Light, on the basis of its load.

Also in 1994, FERC ordered transmission access to the American Electric Power

Company grid to PSI Energy for supply of power to the Blue Ridge Power Agency and four municipalities in Virginia. FERC said that rates, terms and conditions of the imposed transmission service must conform to the agreements between AEP and Blue Ridge.

In late 1994, the Federal Energy Regulatory Commission issued a new transmission pricing policy which encouraged greater pricing flexibility and provided guidance for innovative pricing proposals in the electric utility industry. The policy provides five transmission pricing principles which FERC will follow in approving future transmission proposals:

- Transmission prices must be based on the utility's original embedded costs revenue requirement.

- Any transmission pricing proposal must offer third parties access on the same or comparable basis.

- Transmission pricing should promote economically efficient generation and transmission of electricity.

- Pricing should be fair and equitable.

- Transmission pricing should be practical and easy to administer.

In December 1994, Pacific Gas & Electric Company signed the first wholesale electricity agreement under the Energy Policy Act provision that IPPs have direct access to transmission lines. The agreement with Destec Energy, Inc. (Houston, TX) will permit Destec to sell power directly to the wholesale market in PG&E's territory.

Regional Transmission Groups (RTGs) were created by the Energy Policy Act of 1992 as a method to encourage regional resolution of transmission access issues. In early 1994, the Southwest Power Pool (SPP) announced its intention to ask the FERC to recognize it as a RTG. If created, the Southwest RTG would be the first. The 41 electric company members of SPP in Kansas, Oklahoma, Missouri, Arkansas, Mississippi, Louisiana, Texas, and New Mexico are currently considering the proposal. FERC granted preliminary approval conditioned on the RTG's willingness to accept conditions relating to comparability and joint planning. Later in 1994, a similar preliminary conditional approval for a RTG was given to the Western Regional Transmission Association.

6.3 Short Term Outlook

With the policy to open access to utility transmission systems by FERC, the pace of access agreements is expected to accelerate in 1995. One of the most important issues will be transmission pricing -- determining how to set fair rates for transmission systems.

6.4 Mid-Range and Long Term Outlook

According to William Berry (former chairman of Dominion Power) at the 1994 IEEE Transmission and Distribution Conference (Chicago), utilities are moving toward the creation of seven regional transmission control areas in the United States and Canada. This will be a big change from the 3,000 distribution utility entities currently involved in transmission and distribution. The current structure is excessively fragmented with too many companies, yet too big for one control or centralized management. Part of the transition will be abandonment of cost-of-service pricing and adoption of some form of price-cap regulation in which the utility is permitted to keep money saved through improved efficiency or cost-cutting.

6.5 Opportunities

PUHCA reform merged with emission allowances pooling and increased transmission access will elevate the role and importance of the power pool in marketing, planning, and sales by 2000. This will create increased awareness and understanding of the role of the power pool, the opportunities provided, and the unique regulatory structures under which power pools operate. Power pool planning will be substantially more important and effective than continuing to rely on the unnatural evolution of regional power planning. Owners of sufficient non-utility capacity will ultimately need to be admitted to the power pool for coordination and reliability benefits. A number of existing and new power plants will ultimately sell to the power pool by 2000, rather than to individual electric utility systems, to manage risk, dispatch, and system reliability.

7 RETAIL WHEELING

CONTENTS:

7.1 Trends and Market Assessment
7.2 Recent Activities
7.3 Short Term Outlook
7.4 Mid-Range and Long Term Outlook
7.5 Opportunities

7.1 Trends and Market Assessment

Retail wheeling already exists. ERC, Inc. estimates the current volume at 200 MW to 400 MW.

A 1993 survey of state regulatory commissions by R.J. Rudden Associates, Inc. found that retail wheeling by industrial and/or large commercial customers is currently implemented in only one state, but is expected to experience rapid growth between 1995 and 2000, and beyond 2000.

In 1993, Nevada passed the first retail wheeling law. The legislation was specifically designed to attract North Star Steel Corporation (Minneapolis, MN) to build a new steel mini-mill in the state. The agreement, in effect, allowed the company to buy power on the open market through the grid of the Western Area Power Administration. North Star Steel chose to locate in Arizona, but will still purchase wheeled power.

ERC, Inc. has estimated the market size of retail wheeling at 10,000 MW. The large industrial and commercial retail market potential is limited to the top third of total sales in which electricity prices are at least $0.052 per kWh. It is noted that cogeneration activity to date has generally been associated with utilities having rates above this level.

The Energy Policy Act did not change the current market potential for retail wheeling because FERC is not given authority to issue retail wheeling orders. FERC has made rulings that have permitted retail wheeling in the past. More recently, however, it has refused to do so, limiting itself to voluntary wholesale wheeling conditions in regard to utility mergers and utility applications for market-based pricing of power sales. These conditions are only used to ensure adequate competition within the industry subsequent to mergers and new pricing arrangements. Since FERC will not rule on any retail wheeling request, decisions are left to state PUCs. This formally proscribes state, versus federal, jurisdiction over retail wheeling of electric power.

Outside the United States, retail wheeling is allowed in the United Kingdom and Norway. In Norway, rates have dropped roughly 25% since deregulation in 1991. In the U.K., however, rates have risen by 10%, adjusted for inflation, since 60% of its electric power industry was privatized in 1990. Observers say the increase is because two companies dominate the market.

7.2 Recent Activities

While wholesale wheeling is governed by the Federal Energy Regulatory

Commission, retail wheeling is under the control of each state. Each state can go its own way, and 1994 saw at least three states initiating plans for retail wheeling while at least 20 states, including New York, Connecticut and Texas, appear to be moving toward retail wheeling. Some other states indicated that retail wheeling does not appear to be in their best interest.

The California Public Utilities Commission proposal on retail wheeling was published on 20 April 1994 in *Order Instituting Rulemaking and Order Instituting Investigation*, better known as the *Blue Book*. Pricing would no longed be set by cost of service regulation but through direct access, performance-based regulations where competition exists. Retail wheeling will be phased in, with large commercial and industrial customers entering the competitive market through retail wheeling beginning 01 January 1996. The final stage, including residential customers, would be effective by 01 January 2002. Intermediate dates for direct access are 01 January 1998 for secondary level consumers and 01 January 1999 for all other commercial consumers.

The Michigan Public Service Commission has ordered a five year experimental retail wheeling program. Citing drawbacks in the present system of regulating rates on the basis of a utility's cost of service, as well as retail wheeling's potential benefits to utility customers and the state economy, the Commission ordered that a limited experiment be conducted to determine whether retail wheeling should be adopted in the state on a permanent basis. The Michigan Retail Wheeling Experiment has a five year duration starting whenever Detroit Edison or Consumers Power needs new capacity or seeks to implement a new round of DSM programs. The experiment will involve approximately 1% of each utility's peak demand capacity. Individual customer's participation is limited to between 2 MW and 10 MW of retail delivery capacity at the transmission or sub-transmission voltage level at each location. Retail wheeling customers must assume responsibility for purchasing the power to be delivered to them by the local utility. The Commission said it would decide the price of retail delivery service at a later date. Retail wheeling customers may return to full retail service with their utility at the conclusion of the five year program.

In April 1994, the New York Public Service Commission approved a process for determining how to regulate proposed retail sales to industrial customers by Sithe/Independence Power Partners L.P., the developers of a 1,040 MW natural gas fueled qualifying facility (QF). The Commission had ruled earlier that the proposed retail sales, in the service territory of Niagara Mohawk Power Corporation, would trigger state public utility jurisdiction over the QF. According to the Commission, Sithe must obtain a certificate of public convenience and necessity before it can use its generating facilities to serve retail customers.

The Public Utilities Commission of Ohio confirmed the need for a competitive marketplace in a 1994 report, but no action has been taken. The Industrial Energy Users - Ohio coalition has lobbied to encourage competition in the state.

In August 1994, the Connecticut Department of Public Utility Control temporarily rejected retail wheeling, citing environmental impacts as a primary concern. It was the opinion of the commission that retail wheeling could hamper the timely efforts of Connecticut's utilities to ensure environmental quality. The DPUC issued a draft order in August 1994 stating that if retail wheeling were to be instituted, it should only be implemented when the state is in need of additional capacity. The DPUC stated it would consider the issue of retail wheeling in the future after several issues were resolved. The two largest utilities in Connecticut have indicated that they do not foresee needing additional capacity until approximately 2005.

Concern over the economic impact of retail wheeling in Pennsylvania was expressed by the Pennsylvania Electric Association in comments to the Pennsylvania Public Utility Commission. PEA stated that if retail wheeling were allowed, the utilities' stranded investment could total more than $10 billion. In addition, the state could lose as much as $500 million a year in tax revenue from utilities.

The Vermont Public Service Board has expressed concern regarding the implementation of full-scale retail wheeling in the future. The issue arose in March 1994 during the Board's examination of a series of contracts with Hydro-Quebec for the purchase of interruptible electric power supplies for ski resort snowmaking operations.

On 13 July 1994, PSI Energy announced that it may file a retail wheeling tariff with the Indiana PSC, permitting the company's largest 40 industrial customers to purchase power from alternative suppliers and have PSI wheel the power for them.

The University of Missouri, Columbia Campus, become the first retail electricity end-user to issue a formal request-for-proposal (RFP) for the retail purchase of electricity. The university first negotiated a voluntary retail wheeling agreement with the City of Columbia municipal utility. Electric utilities, power marketers and nonutility generators were invited to submit their bids by 15 December 1994.

One of the biggest deals of the year was an agreement between Detroit Edison Company and each of the Big Three automakers which reduced rates for the three companies in exchange for guarantees that they will remain utility customers and abandon cogeneration for 10 years. The agreement was viewed as a smart move by Detroit Edison to keep its biggest customers from participating in the retail wheeling market. General Motors expects to save about $10 million in annual utility costs while Chrysler predicts savings of about $20 million. The contracts with each of the three automakers were identical.

7.3 Short Term Outlook

An important event to watch will be the selection of a power supplier by the University of Missouri, Columbia Campus on 15 January 1995, in the first retail wheeling deal completed through a formal request-for-proposal process. The procedure of negotiating a voluntary retail wheeling agreement with an electric utility and purchasing power through an RFP will probably be replicated throughout the United States. Agreements and RFPs will serve as the initial mechanism for retail wheeling in lieu of mandated retail wheeling because of the more-distant deadlines by which state commissions will phase in forced retail wheeling.

Several more states will initiate plans for retail wheeling. Other states are expected formally postpone any actions.

New Jersey has announced that it will formally investigate retail wheeling in 1995. In a draft master plan released on 16 November 1994, New Jersey's Board of

Public Utilities published Phase I of a proposed scheme that would open all supply of new electric capacity and competition. Phase II will investigate retail wheeling, whether existing power plants are in danger of being rendered useless by wholesale competition.

The Washington Utilities & Transmission Commission is in the process of taking public comment, and announced its intention to begin developing new rules that could allow retail wheeling in the state. The interest in retail wheeling is being driven by several large industrial companies, including Boeing Company, Weyerhaeuser Corporation, Longview Fibre, and Georgia Pacific Corporation.

A bill to allow retail competition died in the New Mexico legislature in 1993. Proponents believe a similar bill could pass in 1995.

A major controversy associated with the Michigan plan for retail wheeling is the price utilities would be paid for wheeling power. The prices proposed by opposing groups ranged from $0.005 to $0.05 per kW. A decision by the Michigan Commission is expected in early 1995.

7.4 Mid-Range and Long Term Outlook

Electric Light & Power reported that a panel of experts at the 1994 Edison Electric Institute Financial Conference (San Diego, CA) concluded that retail wheeling is moving further into the future, predicting retail wheeling five or more years down the road. This is in contrast to the 1993 meeting, where the consensus seemed to be that retail wheeling was imminent.

Some serious issues have to be dealt with before retail wheeling can take off in the United States. Foremost is that electric utilities have an estimated $200 billion to $300 billion worth of power plants that are not efficient enough to compete in an open market, especially against newer plants that use efficient, combined-cycle gas turbines. How to compensate utilities for this stranded investment is the subject of much debate today. Another issue is that larger customers would have more clout in negotiating deals than smaller ones.

In a June 1994 editorial in *Electric Light & Power*, editor M.T. Hoske observed that many view retail wheeling as a Pandora's Box that should never be opened. The argument is that once one state has retail wheeling, other states would have to allow their businesses an equal opportunity for lower energy costs. Opponents fear widespread utility bankruptcies, decimation of demand-side management (DSM) and environmental programs, and lower reliability. Without a smooth transition to competition, high-cost utilities with captive ratepayers could incur huge losses as they drop rates to match those of lower-cost suppliers. Without enough revenue to support existing expenses and debt payments, balance sheet write-downs and net-income losses may occur. This has already caused many utilities to make huge efforts in cutting costs in recent years.

According to *Overview of Issues Relating to the Retail Wheeling of Electricity*, published by the National Regulatory Research Institute (Washington, DC), widespread acceptance of retail wheeling by policy makers may take several years, due in part to the inability to correctly measure potential costs. Overall, the broad effects of retail wheeling include benefits that would not be identified until several years down the road and even then they would be indirect and difficult to measure. From a long-term perspective, retail wheeling could radically change the structure, operation and performance of the electric power industry. The industry could see vertical disintegration of utilities that do not perceive themselves as high value producers, the breakdown of the "regulatory compact," a transformation of the integrated resource planning process and fundamental changes in state regulation of service where customers have rights and the ability to shop around.

7.5 Opportunities

Six major long-term gains of retail wheeling include: more efficient utility pricing, more efficient utility operations and investments, more appropriate "regulatory compact," more efficient industry structure, reduced price differentials among electric utilities, and stronger U.S. economy and promotion of economic development.

8 INTERNATIONAL ACTIVITIES

CONTENTS:

8.1 Trends and Market Assessment
8.2 Recent Activities
8.3 Short Term Outlook
8.4 Mid-Range and Long Term Outlook
8.5 Opportunities

8.1 Trends and Market Assessment

International markets represent a promising new opportunity for United States utilities and energy development companies to utilize the skills developed in this country. The regulatory burdens on international developers were substantially reduced with the passage of the Energy Policy Act of 1992. In addition to the construction of electric power plants and the operation of independent power or privatized facilities, there are substantial opportunities for products and services related to energy conservation. The benefits of demand side management are now beginning to be recognized worldwide.

The worldwide export market for power generation, oil and gas production equipment, and energy efficient equipment is projected to total $1.6 trillion by 2010.

According to RCG/Hagler Bailly, Inc. (Arlington, VA), as of mid-1993, there were

787 independent power projects under development in 59 countries, totalling 359,346

MW. The distribution is as follows:

- Latin America: 159 initiatives, 18 countries, 38,521 MW
- Europe: 195 initiatives, 21 countries, 68,198 MW
- Asia: 433 initiatives, 20 countries, 258,277 MW

The distribution of these projects by fuel type is:

- Coal: 43% by capacity, 26% of projects
- Hydro: 20% by capacity, 16% of projects
- Natural gas: 23% by capacity, 31% of projects
- Other: 14% by capacity, 27% of projects

Competition in private power projects abroad involves a variety of entities. There

are over 115 active "players", seven large and local engineering and construction firms,

and 15 industrial conglomerates in pursuit of this massive opportunity. Thirty equipment

suppliers and 30 U.S. developers add further competitive pressure. Foreign electric

utility subsidiaries (12), and international and local fuel suppliers (12) offer additional

services toward fulfilling demand for power.

The leading IPPs are active in over 50 countries: 34 of them in Mexico, 26 in

China, 18 in Argentina, 17 in the U.K., 16 in India, 14 in the Philippines, 11 in

Australia, and 11 in Germany.

8.2 Recent Activities

During 1994, most U.S. power developers focused their attention on developing

countries in Asia and Latin America. While suitability for private power projects in some

countries declined, prospects in other countries have become more promising. Prospects for power project financing improved in Pakistan, for example, as utilities moved to arrange letters of credit. In China, however, utilities were unwilling to provide any guarantees for performance.

Despite the emerging demand, 1994 was a buyers market for power plant construction in Asia. According to a presentation by Thomas Kalin, Black & Veatch International, at Power-Gen Asia, a new coal-fired power plant can be ordered in Asia for 35% to 40% less than the going rate in the United States market a few years ago. Everybody involved in supplying new capacity to the Asian market has cut prices. Steam turbines are 40% cheaper. Engineering costs are 40% lower. Methods are being found to shave construction schedules by 40%. It is definitely a buyers market in Asia.

On 4 February 1994, President Clinton lifted the 19-year embargo on U.S. trade with Vietnam. Vietnam plans to invest over $4 billion in power development by 2000 and has an immediate need of high, medium, and low-tension transmission lines. The government is inviting foreign companies to invest in its programs. A Japanese joint venture of Nippon Koei and EPDC recently won a contract to design twin hydropower plants that will be built with $600 million in aid from the Japanese government.

The announcement of four major projects in India was made in mid-1994. The largest is a $12 billion, 10,560 MW coal-fired plant to be developed by Consolidated Electric Power Asia, Ltd. The plant is planned to be in full operation by 2000.

Indonesia's national electric utility, Perushann Listrik Negara, has approved construction of coal-fired private power projects that may produce a total of 9,000 MW. The deals are part of the race by the Indonesian government to provide generating capacity to meet growing industrial demand. The country's plan calls for 27,500 MW of new generating capacity to be built over the next 10 to 12 years, mostly by private developers. A project at Tanjung Jati, to be developed by Consolidated Electric Power Asia, a subsidiary of Hopewell Holdings, Ltd. will involve up to 4,000 MW. Another project will be the 1,230 MW coal-fired Paiton powerplant to be developed by Mission Energy Company at a cost of $2.6 billion.

Wing Group, Ltd. (Woodlands, TX) announced in September 1994 a 2,400 MW gas-fired generating plant in China's Jiangsu Providence. Wing-led groups have also won approval from China's Ministry of Electric Power to develop two other 2,400 MW gas-fired plants and three coal-burning plants costing a total of about $8 billion.

The U.S. Departments of Energy and Commerce sponsored a U.S. Electric Power Technologies Seminar and Mission to Seoul, Korea in October 1994. The purpose was to assist U.S. firms begin exploiting the large potential market for U.S. power generation equipment, technology and services which will develop over the next decade.

The first government permit to build private power plant in Mexico was granted in March 1994. A consortium led by Southern Electric International, Inc. will build a 225 MW, $230 million cogeneration plant near Monterrey.

In early 1994, the Italian government announced plans to privatize its electrical supply by the end of the year. In sweeping new laws, the Italian Parliament abolished government pricing. ENEL, the former Italian Electricity Board, became a wholly owned government corporation, and will soon change even more as ENEL stock is sold off to private buyers.

Japan opened retail wheeling in December 1994, when the Ministry of International Trade and Industries set up a new system allowing companies to sell excess electric power on the retail market.

The 1994 Cogeneration/IPP Production Survey by the Association of Energy Engineers (Atlanta, GA), showed 61% of members felt that the best markets for cogeneration and independent power products and repowering were international, and not in the United States. Following is the distribution of where survey participants believe the best market are:

- Latin America: 29%
- Europe: 29%
- Asia: 24%
- Russia: 8%
- Middle East: 6%
- China: 4%

8.3 Short Term Outlook

The best opportunities for U.S. industry are in Indonesia, Columbia, China, Argentina and India, according to a presentation at the Cogen Turbo Power Congress and Exposition (Atlanta, GA) by M. Chiesa of the Sumitomo Bank, Ltd. Columbia and Argentina are developing extensive natural gas infrastructures. India will require approximately 40,000 MW of power in the next 15 years. China's coastal provinces will need 25% to 38% more power for the next several years.

China's independent power market is the world's largest according to RCC/Hagler Bailly, Inc. (Arlington, VA). There are several independently developed plants operating, 60 under development, and about 64 in preliminary stages. They total about 188,000

MW. According to *Power Engineering*, new generating capacity is being added in China now at the rate of 10 GW to 15 GW per year; this rate is expected to increase. It is estimated that Chinese industrial output is being inhibited by about 20% due to shortages of electric power.

According to *Power Engineering* (November 1994), there are at least a dozen other rapidly growing economies in Asia that need new power, in addition to China. The situation is the same as that in China, but to a lesser extent, in the other developing Asian countries.

According to Utility Data Institute (Washington, DC), the countries of Latin America and the Caribbean could increase their installed capacity by over 65,000 MW through 2009. This will constitute a 40% increase in capacity, about two-thirds of which is already under construction. Approximately 37% of the new capacity will be in Brazil, with Mexico and Argentina both adding about 15% of the total 65,000 MW. Venezuela should add about 9,240 MW, and the remainder of the capacity will come from Peru, Chile, Colombia, Ecuador, Uruguay, Panama, and Cuba. About 65% of the projected additions are hydro projects, with the remainder being oil-fired, coal, natural gas, and nuclear projects.

Political and economic changes have had dramatic impacts on the utility industry throughout Europe. Even before these enormous changes, demand for electrical power in western Europe was growing at a steady pace (in excess of 3.5% per year since 1989). Power producers in the European Countries (EC) now forecast a total of 86,000 MW of new generating capacity through 2000. Of this total, less than half is currently under construction. Electrical power currently flows from west to east in Europe, however, experts believe this trend will reverse itself in the future as Eastern Europe becomes more willing to accept new power plant construction. The 1992 annual sales of equipment throughout Eastern Europe exceed $4 billion. This figure is expected to climb to over $7 billion annually by 1997.

8.4 Mid-Range and Long Term Outlook

According to RCG/Hagler Bailly, Inc., the international opportunities for independent power are huge:

- Power plants: $700 to $800 billion worth of new facilities will be needed by 2000.

- Transmission and distribution: Expansion of services will require an additional $300 billion to $400 billion.

- Repowering and improving existing plants: The estimate is $40 billion to $60 billion.

Massive growth is expected in non-North American power between 1993 to 2000:

- Asia: 365 GW
- Europe: 142 GW
- Latin America: 74 GW
- Middle East: 33 GW
- Africa: 32 GW

Of these 646 GW, 479 GW will be in developing countries. Of the 167 GW in developed countries, 95 GW will be in Europe and 72 GW in Asia.

According to Utility Data Institute, projected electric capacity additions worldwide from 1993 through 2002 are estimated to be around 550 GW, of which 45% is in Asia.

This increase of 19% over the installed worldwide base of some 2,905 GW now in-service equates to an annual increase of 1.9% per year from 1987 through 1991, despite the huge increases planned in China particularly, and Asia generally over the next decade.

On a regional basis, capacity in the 10 year block is distributed as follows:

- Asia: 244 GW
- Russia and the CIS: 20 GW
- The European Union: 77 GW
- Other Europe: 15 GW
- Latin America: 51 GW
- The Middle East: 30 GW
- North America: 94 GW
- The rest of the world: 15 GW

The 1993 through 2002 block of new capacity has a varied fuel mix with 25% coal-fired, 21% gas-fired, 22% hydroelectric, 13% nuclear, 8% oil-fired, and 11% using a dozen other fuels or renewable resources.

Over the next twenty years, 1,330 gigawatts will be required. This will result in a total utility investment of $2.6 trillion between 1993 and 2012. Transmission and distribution investments will total $1 trillion and generation $900 billion.

An optimistic long-range international market forecast was presented at the opening session of the 1994 IEEE T&D conference in Chicago by Hans Weinrich, president of IEEE's Power Engineering Society and vice president of ABB's T&D Division. He said the total world power market for generation, transmission, distribution, and associated goods and services will require investment of $2.6 trillion between 1991 and 2010. That includes $900 billion on generation and $1 trillion on T&D. The generation market will require 1330 GW of new capacity to be constructed between 1991 and 2010 in the following geographic areas: 15% in the U.S., 20% in OECD (developed) countries except for the U.S., 18% in Eastern Europe and the CIS countries, and 47% in 100 developing countries in Asia, South America, and Africa.

The European Wind Energy Association (Rome, Italy) predicts creation of over 11,500 MW of new wind generation capacity in Britain, Denmark, Germany and the Netherlands by 2005. Longer-term European plans are for 100,000 MW by 2030.

8.5 Opportunities

According to Arthur Andersen & Company (New York, NY) and Cambridge Energy Research Associates, Inc. (Cambridge, MA), the idea of a truly global power company is becoming a reality. Even as the United States and other developed economies continue to electrify throughout the 1990s, much of the world has barely begun the process. As generating, transmission, and distribution facilities are built and operated to satisfy these needs, an important role for global companies translating local or regionally acquired skills and knowledge into widely dispersed business centers is expected.

While the Energy Policy Act allows new competition within the territories of U.S. utilities, it also allows them easier means to expand internationally.

Virtually every major utility is now at least exploring these potential international opportunities. For example, Southern Company, one of the U.S's three largest utilities, is very interested in foreign business. In 1992, it bought a 50% stake in Freeport Power

Company (Bahamas). The company has considered opportunities in China, Hong Kong, Mexico, Chile, and Argentina.

In the Commonwealth of Independent States, U.S. partners include: Cincinnati Gas & Electric Company, which is paired with Kazakhstan's state energy company Kazakhstanenergo; the National Hydropower Association, paired with Kyrgyzstan State Energy Company, which generates 70% of its energy from hydro; and the American Gas Association with GAZPROM, Russia's natural gas company, and ROSGAZ, Russia's gas distribution company. Partnerships on the horizon include the City of Pasadena Public Utility Department and Southern California Edison Company with Armenia and General Public Utilities Corporation and Wisconsin Power & Light Company in Ukraine.

9 DEMAND-SIDE MANAGEMENT

CONTENTS:

9.1 Trends and Market Assessment
9.2 Recent Activities
9.3 Short Term Outlook
9.4 Mid-Range and Long Term Outlook
9.5 Opportunities

9.1 Trends and Market Assessment

According to the Energy Information Administration, based on responses by electric utilities to its Form EIA-861, electric utilities spent $2.36 billion on demand-side management (DSM) in 1992, cut energy use by 31,800 GWh, and cut potential peak demand by 32,900 MW. Compared to national totals for the electric utility industry, DSM accounted for 1.3% of retail sales, 1.3% of retail revenues, and 6.0% of peak demand. Of 1992 expenditures, almost 80% was for direct program costs, with the remaining 20% for indirect costs. Almost 2/3 of these costs were devoted to energy efficiency programs. Program costs have been increasing, from $1.75 billion in 1991 to $1.18 billion in 1990.

According to *Drivers of Electricity Growth and the Role of Utility Demand-Side Management*, published by EPRI, DSM and energy-efficiency measures are slowing the rate of electricity sales growth. According to EPRI manager of DSM program design Paul Meagher, U.S. electricity sales, which increased at about 68 billion kWh per year between 1960 and 1990, will slow to about 46 BkWh per year by 2010. Although customer growth and economic factors will produce annual gains of 79 BkWh, these will be offset by decreases of 22 BkWh/year from efficiency and 11 BkWh/year from DSM.

Important motivating forces for U.S. electric utilities to engage in DSM planning are state regulatory commissions. A number of states have recently passed regulations requiring that DSM resources be treated equally (or even preferentially) with supply resources. Other states are in the process of passing similar regulations.

According to a 1993 survey by EPRI of 734,000 participants in commercial utility DSM programs, the following practices were utilized:

- Lighting: 240,255 participants (32.7%)
- Audit/building envelope: 113,092 participants (15.4%)
- HVAC: 88,713 participants (12.1%)
- Special rates: 83,970 participants (11.4%)
- Load control: 71,545 participants (9.8%)
- Miscellaneous/informational: 55,849 participants (7.6%)
- Efficient appliances: 37,092 participants (5.1%)
- Motors/drives: 9,650 participants (1.3%)
- Thermal storage: 1,429 participants (0.2%)
- Standby generation: 279 participants (0.03)

The same EPRI survey of 145,000 industrial participants found the following practices:

- Special rates: 64,688 participants (44.6%)
- Lighting: 25,210 participants (17.4%)
- Motors/drives: 14,516 participants (10.0%)
- Audit/building envelope: 14,147 participants (9.8%)
- Efficient appliances: 12,408 participants (8.6%)
- Miscellaneous/informational: 11,349 participants (7.8%)

- Load control: 3,273 participants (2.3%)
- HVAC: 3,094 participants (2.1%)
- Thermal storage: 243 participants (0.2%)
- Standby generation: 219 participants (0.2%)

A survey of the American Public Power Association found the following percentages of utilities with various DSM program features for the residential sector:

- Energy audits: 50%
- Load management: 48%
- Water heating: 43%
- New construction: 35%
- HVAC/heat pumps: 32%
- Lighting: 31%
- Building efficiency: 24%
- Incentive rates: 21%
- Appliances: 20%
- Shade tree planting: 13%

A 1994 study by DynCorp-Meridian for the National Renewable Energy Laboratory found that 22 of 50 states had DSM statutes, either directing the utility commissions to consider DSM, to implement DSM policies, or to allow cost recovery of DSM programs.

Lawrence Berkeley Laboratory published a report in 1994 on DSM bidding contracts. As of October 1993, utilities had selected over 170 bids for about 425 MWs of demand reductions. Levelized total resource costs range between $0.054 and $0.08 per kWh, with payments to bidders accounting for 70% to 90% of total program costs.

9.2 Recent Activities

A dramatic change was observed in utility DSM programs in 1994. In a front-page story, November 1994, *Energy User News* reported that "Uncertainties Lead Utilities to Retreat from Rebates." In moves that could foreshadow the future of demand-side management, pressure from large customers, increasing competitiveness in the electric utility industry, mixed messages from regulators and government, and uncertainty about tax liabilities have motivated three major utilities to curtail or eliminate their rebate programs. EUN reported that efforts by Niagara Mohawk Power Corporation (Syracuse, NY), Southern California Edison Company (Rosemead, CA), and Pacific Gas and Electric Company (PG&E - San Francisco, CA) to reduce or eliminate the role of rebates in their DSM programs are being closely watched by end users, regulators, and DSM program managers. All three companies were national leaders in the rebate movement that swept the utility industry a few years ago.

The value of demand-side management appeared to fall in favor in the view of utility executives in 1994. A 1994 survey by Washington International Energy Group (Washington, DC) asked 285 senior U.S. utility executives to rank 23 issues on a scale of importance. Demand-side management ranked 18th on the list, with only 14% of respondents rating it "very important." In 1992, 74% said they believed DSM was effective, but only 55% agreed with the statement in 1994. Also, only 41% now view DSM as a long-term alternative to building new generation, while 51% don't see it as a good alternative. Furthermore, 38% of 1994 respondents think of DSM as merely a way to appease regulators, an increase from 28% in 1993.

Pacific Gas & Electric asked the California PUC for a $100 million reduction in authorized spending on electric DSM programs as part of its 1995 electric rate freeze.

Total electric and gas spending in 1995 will be $150 million, down from the $180 million estimated 1994 expenditure, and the $280 million originally authorized for 1995. PG&E is under strong pressure to reduce rates and is gradually moving its DSM programs to emphasize information and participant funding.

Baltimore Gas & Electric proposed changes in rebate levels of three of its major conservation programs, reflecting the utility's desire to pursue conservation with a "focus on the creative use of market forces as opposed to the current highly prescriptive central planning approach."

Entergy Corporation has petitioned the Arkansas Public Service Commission to reconcile rules for demand-side management as well as IRP.

Louisiana Power & Light Company asked the Louisiana Public Service Commission to withdraw DSM action programs filed in 1992.

Detroit Edison has petitioned the Michigan Public Service Commission to revise their DSM program by authorizing only those efficiency options that pass the Ratepayer Impact Measure (RIM), augmented by certain measures that add value for customers. In January 1994, the PSC increased the utility's DSM three-year target expenditures. At the risk of penalties, Detroit Edison has budgeted below these levels. In an interview with *Demand-Side Monthly*, a spokesperson for Detroit Edison was quoted as saying "the penalty, coupled with new competitive threats, merely contribute to the utility's long-standing opposition to energy efficiency programs."

Eric Hirst of Oak Ridge National Laboratory, in analyzing data from 1993 EIA-861 forms, points out that, while some utilities in the Northeast and California are cutting back on their DSM programs, utilities in other parts of the country began new DSM programs or increased existing programs.

Speaking to the 1994 ACEEE Summer Study meeting, Richard Sonstelie, president and CEO of Puget Power & Light Company said that one of the most troubling ramifications of the recent changes in the electric utility industry is the tendency to abandon utility efforts in demand-side management. He warned of "stranded DSM investments" and advised DSM advocates to get creative in their DMS programs. Regulators, taking their cues from their peers, are showing signs of responding to pressure to avoid rate increases. For his utility, Sonstelie said, immediate recovery of DSM expenditures, including carrying costs, was more important than decoupling.

In addressing a 19 September 1994 ADSMP National Capital Meeting, James Dobson, vice president of Donaldson, Lufkin & Jenrette, said that there is an economically justified level of DSM, but it is much less than the current level of activity. With the transition to a competitive environment occurring even faster than predicted, the result will be that the basic tenets of DSM must be questioned.

In conjunction with its annual Utility Rebate Guide, *Energy User News (EUN)* also assesses current trends in the DSM field. In conjunction with its May 1994 review, a number of utility sources told EUN that the early success of rebate programs, as gauged by the number of end user applications filed, has prompted energy providers to cut rebate levels. Typically targeting lighting programs, some utility companies have halved rebates while maintaining program budgets. Such moves, the companies argue, encourage more end users to invest in energy management for the same utility expenditure in rebates.

At the same time, 1994 saw the wide-spread initiation of DSM financing programs. By offering shared savings contracts either through demand-side management departments or private energy service companies, utility companies are increasing the end user's responsibility in funding energy management projects. In many cases, utility companies now offer financing in conjunction with rebates, however.

While increasing the end user's financial responsibility, many utility companies also require increased end user accountability for energy management projects. The incorporation of audit requirements into DSM programs is often accompanied by improved audit services, new funding for audits, and pre-qualification of auditors by utilities for end users.

Other shifts in demand-side management programs are a shift from consumption-driven to demand-driven programs and the growth in the number of load-building programs offered by both fuel and power companies.

In 1994, the Results Center and IRT Environment (Aspen, CO) reported four of the most successful U.S. load management programs:

- TU Electric's thermal cool storage program, the largest U.S. program of its kind, has 205 installations.

- Florida Power Corporation gets 700 MW load reduction on demand from nearly half a million customers, or 44%, who accept a monthly credit to curtail heavy load appliances.

- Buckeye Power gives customers a demand-charge discount to install radio controls and has hooked up 82,000 water heaters and 2,800 electric space heaters.

- United Power Association (Elk River, MN) uses a variety of incentives to cut electric load including lower rates, reduced demand charges and rebates.

A 1994 study by E. Hirst and S. Hadley at Oak Ridge National Laboratory concluded that although electric utility demand-side management programs may reduce overall electric bills, they typically increase prices slightly over lifetimes of the measures installed. The effects on prices are rather small -- probably in the range of 2% nationally. The study gives ammunition to those who have challenged aggressive DSM programs as causing rate increases.

9.3 Short Term Outlook

Despite the cutback in rebates, some utilities will expand their DSM programs. PECO Energy Company will expand its DSM program in 1995. In compliance with an order issued by the Pennsylvania Utilities Commission, the utility will commit an additional $10 million, above the amount currently reflected in base rates in 1995. New DSM programs will include:

- Residential lighting
- Residential house decor
- Residential HVAC incentives
- Residential energy efficient new construction
- Commercial audits/surveys
- Audits for large commercial and industrial customers

There is a major effort to increase the effectiveness of existing DSM programs for many utilities. According to a study by the American Council for an Energy-Efficient Economy (Washington, DC), among incentive-based DSM programs, the most successful programs have achieved more than two times the participation and roughly six times the electricity savings as a percentage of industrial sales as the average program. Some industrial DSM programs which were modeled after commercial programs have not been particularly successful. Industrial customers want to know how to improve the productivity of their facilities, not simply how to improve their energy efficiency. Changes can be expected in 1995 in programs which have not yet achieved the desired results.

9.4 Mid-Range and Long Term Outlook

Based on responses by utility's to Form EIA-861, utilities expect their expenditures to increase in 1997 to $4 billion (in 1993 dollars), or 1.8% of revenues. Energy savings and potential peak demand reductions are expected to reach 72,800 GWh and 49,500 MW, respectively, in 1997. However, one must view the results of this survey in light of the very major changes which took place within the past year.

The future path of demand-side management programs is obscured in a haze of important questions regarding retail wheeling, legislation, and other issues. As pointed out by Robert Smock in a November 1994 editorial in *Electric Light & Power*, "Survivors of ruthless competition will not be doing much to reduce electricity sales. They'll be doing their best to sell their product." This opinion was backed by Jeremy Bloom, manager of the DSM business unit at EPRI. In an interview in *Electric Light & Power* (January 1995), he said, "As electric markets move toward greater competition, it will be difficult for utilities to implement DSM in the same way as in the past."

At a 1994 meeting of the Utility Purchasing Management Group, Don Hodel, managing director of Summit Group International, said he foresees that full-scale retail wheeling will terminate utility demand-side management programs. According to Hodel, full-blown, flat-out competition in the retail electricity market will force the players to ruthlessly eliminate cost, including activities that do not make economic sense.

Most utilities believe rebate programs will continue, but they see them constantly evolving. Even with budget cuts, programs will not be eliminated. Many DSM programs are required by state utility commissions as part of integrated resource planning requirements. In the face of competition, customer service is of increasing importance, and utilities recognize that DSM programs are excellent for customer relationships.

Conventional wisdom seems to be that rebates on certain technologies will diminish as markets become established, and in fact, is already happening. The New England Electric System, which spends the highest percent of its revenues on DSM of any utility in the country, reports they have been so successful with lighting rebates they are ready to shift their program emphasis to other technologies, such as motors and HVAC. In essence, the emphasis will soon change from "just finding ways to save energy" to more sophisticated manipulations of the energy-efficiency marketplace. With the billions of dollars a year of ratepayer money to use, utilities are going to have a major influence in that marketplace.

9.5 Opportunities

According to Sam Barakat, president of Barakat & Chamberlin (Oakland, CA), one of the results of the Energy Act will be significant utility diversification into demand-side management related services. Utilities will create unregulated subsidiaries to provide

DSM and related services outside their own service territories, similar to the way many utility affiliates are currently developing supply side facilities for other utilities. Two examples are New England Power and Boston Edison, which have recently established energy service subsidiaries. The trend will be for utilities to become more sophisticated in providing services, and much more service-oriented in general.

This increasing service orientation could assist utilities in retaining large industrial customers that currently constitute a large portion of their rate base. Several large utilities, such as Virginia Power, have recently announced their intention to develop cogeneration facilities for large industrial customers within their own service territories. By doing so, they are attempting to reclaim a market that had been conceded to non-utility developers. Large industrial customers will become much more sophisticated in their attempts to reach more innovative service arrangements with power supplies.

Some utilities contract their DSM program to energy service companies (ESCOs), who offer to reduce demand or energy by a specified number of kilowatts or kilowatt hours. The term ESCO is most commonly used to refer to utility industry contractors performing or promising to perform a variety of DSM-related tasks. In a typical arrangement, the ESCO is responsible for finding customers within the utility's service territory and achieving the demand reduction goal. This is done by implementing programs such as replacing energy intensive lighting, motor, or cooling systems with more energy-efficient systems, or by shifting energy demand to off-peak periods. The utility pays the ESCO on the basis of performance, with many contracts including bonuses, penalties, or both for exceeding or failing to meet the goal. The ESCO might also receive payments from the customer based on realized energy cost savings. The ESCO industry is likely to experience strong growth through the middle of the decade, after which there could be some industry consolidation.

Third-party "bidding" is one way to obtain DSM resources. In a DSM bidding program, utilities solicit proposals for projects from customers and ESCOs. DSM bidding is an auction in which a utility generally solicits proposals from ESCOs interested in achieving specified amounts of DSM savings (e.g., 1,000 kW of demand reduction). There are many variations on the theme. Eligible bidders can include ESCOs that develop projects with utility customers on an energy performance contracting or "shared savings" basis, other vendors, or the utility's own customers. Bids can be structured as the price to supply a block of kW demand reductions, kWh energy savings, or both.

According to Lawrence Berkeley Laboratory, ESCOs were responsible for about 87% of over 170 DSM bidding contracts awarded by U.S. utilities as of October 1994. A number of ESCOs have developed a limited national presence through their involvement in utility bidding programs. Currently, the DSM bidding market is not dominated by firms that are utility affiliates of subsidiaries.

According to Arthur Andersen & Company (New York, NY) and Cambridge Energy Research Associates, Inc. (Cambridge, MA), by the end of the decade, there may still be a role for specialized DSM contractors, however, by then, it is equally probable the dominant ESCOs will include the electricity suppliers, utilities, and NUGs that have come to understand the needs of highly differentiated power markets and have responded to those needs.

10 ENERGY CONSERVATION EQUIPMENT AND SERVICES

CONTENTS:

10.1 Trends and Market Assessment
10.2 Recent Activities
10.3 Short Term Outlook
10.4 Mid-Range and Long Term Outlook
10.5 Opportunities

10.1 Trends and Market Assessment

There are several primary market drivers which make the 1990s an unprecedented time in history for business opportunities in energy management and energy conservation. These include utility demand-side management programs, increased global competitiveness for U.S. industry, new programs for energy conservation in facilities operated by the federal government, increased awareness and implementation of energy conservation by building designers and contractors, new mandatory national and state standards, and voluntary efforts such as EPA's Green Lights program.

According to the Energy Information Administration, U.S. industries spent $102.3 billion on energy in 1990. According to Future Technology Surveys, Inc. (Lilburn, GA), U.S. industry spends $10 billion on energy management and energy conservation annually.

According to same sources, commercial buildings spend over $80 billion on energy annually, and spend about $7 billion on energy management and energy conservation in commercial buildings annually.

The federal government is the single largest energy consumer in the world. It has been estimated that federal energy efficiency programs now being put in place will save up to $1 billion annually. The federal government occupies more than 500,000 buildings worldwide, 80% of which are owned and operated by the U.S. Department of Defense. More than 40% of total annual energy expenditures are directly related to heating, cooling and lighting federal buildings, according to the Congressional Office of Technology Assessment. Of the $10 billion spent annually by the federal government on energy, about 40% or $4 billion is expended annually for electricity, natural gas, and other energy sources to operate federal buildings. The other 60% goes to gasoline and transportation fuels, as well as industrial process energy.

According to the U.S. Energy Information Administration, residential energy expenditures are more than $110 billion annually. Progress has been made in residential energy conservation in the past decade. The typical home built in 1970 uses at least 35% more energy than a comparable home built in 1990, mainly due to the increased insulation standards, improved mechanical efficiencies and building standards incorporating such considerations such as appliance energy use and air-conditioning.

According to the Office of Technology Assessment (OTA), implementation of existing technologies could save U.S. citizens and businesses $80 billion annually on energy bills.

The most zealous advocates of energy conservation programs, such as Amory Lovins of the Rocky Mountain Institute (Old Snowmass, CO), have estimated the United States could cut energy consumption by as much as 75% and avoid the need to build any new power plants for decades.

The Department of Energy (DoE) and the Environmental Protection Agency have joined forces for the development of a voluntary, industry-driven, collaborative program called Motor Challenge. The program is aimed at assisting U.S. business and industry through showcase demonstrations designed for multiple industry teams to demonstrate efficient electric motor systems at specific facilities. The program will involve soliciting industry partners at a corporate level, or at specific industrial facilities, to make upgrades. It will allow for the provision of expert technical and organizational support and training to industry participants, and will serve as promoter for EMS benchmarks. Other participants in the program include the National Electrical Manufacturers Association, The National Association of Manufacturers, Edison Electric Institute, and Electric Power Research Institute. The DoE has stated that the Motor Challenge program has the potential of saving U.S. industries as much as $3 billion annually by 2000 and nearly $13 billion annually by 2010.

According to Newton-Evans Research Company (Ellicott City, MO), electric utilities spent more than $350 million on energy management systems in 1994. EMS operations will concentrate on the development and implementation of advanced security applications, especially optimal power flow, network topology, state estimation, and operator load flow.

According to the United States Environmental Protection Agency, lighting accounts for 20% to 25% of the electricity used in the United States. Technologies now exist to reduce lighting energy usage by 75% or more. According to EPA, installation of energy efficient lighting can cut lighting electricity usage by 50%, freeing $18.6 billion from rate payer bills for investment and allowing $60 billion of capital to be invested in new jobs, rather than new power plants. The EPA Green Lights Program has been enormously successful in encouraging major U.S. companies to install energy efficient lighting. The goal is to reduce the demand for electricity, and thereby, reduce greenhouse gas emissions.

For virtually the first time in the era of modern air conditioning factors external to or distinct from the building's thermal requirements are having, and will continue to have, a major impact on HVAC design and on the directors and pace of change. External environmental issues are major forces for change in HVAC system design and technology, particularly the following:

- The impact and regulation of chlorofluorocarbons and power plant emissions

- Electric utilities' capacity problems and resulting strategies to increase energy efficiency and shift demand off-peak

- Heightened concerns, lawsuits, and potential liabilities related to "sick building syndrome" and other indoor air quality problems

- The tremendous expansion in HVAC design options and system integration capabilities made possible by direct digital control technology

Electric utilities, through their rate and incentive strategies to reduce peak load and shift demand off-peak, have stimulated and continue to spur important changes in

HVAC systems and trends. The best known, perhaps, is ice thermal storage by which users achieve significant reductions in energy operating cost.

The impact of computers and electronics on the HVAC industry has revolutionized the way building systems are designed, controlled, and monitored. DDC systems and equipment controls provide an unprecedented capability to monitor and control HVAC systems, making them more responsive to building conditions. The ability to monitor system parameters and gather and analyze data on a continuous basis is a powerful tool for real-time optimization and for a much better understanding of the dynamics of an operating building.

The United States spends approximately $70 billion annually to operate commercial and industrial buildings. Now, a wide variety of energy-efficient technologies can cut this energy use by more than 40%. That amounts to $28 billion that can be reinvested in the economy each year, rather than wasted on unnecessary electricity use. This profitable and efficient use of energy also means less air pollution.

Lighting accounts for 20% to 25% of all electricity use in the United States. If everyone in the country used energy-efficient lighting, the nation could save about $16 billion per year, and could reduce carbon dioxide, nitrogen oxides, and sulfur dioxide emissions from utilities by up to 12%.

The Energy Star Buildings program is a five-stage process in which EPA asks participants to perform energy-efficiency upgrades only where profitable. The program starts with membership in Green Lights, followed by a comprehensive building survey and tune-up. It then calls for reducing heating, ventilation, and air conditioning (HVAC) loads and improving fans and air-handling systems. The program finishes with an improved HVAC plant, comprised of more efficient chiller and heating systems.

EPA has also developed the Energy Star Computer program, a partnership with leading computer manufacturers to develop desktop computers, monitors, and printers that can "sleep" or "power-down," when not in use. Computers currently account for 5% of commercial electricity consumption. As the fastest growing business electricity load, this could rise to 10% by 2000. As many as 30% to 40% of personal computers are left running at night and on weekends.

10.2 Recent Activities

On 08 March 1994, President Clinton signed Federal Order 12902, the *Federal Energy and Water Efficiency Executive Order*. The Executive Order is designed to meet an exceed provisions for federal energy and water efficiency that were contained in the Energy Policy Act of 1992, which mandated that agencies reduce energy consumption in federal buildings 20% by 2000 from 1985 levels. This order will exceed that goal and cut energy use in federal buildings by 30% by the year 2005 over 1985 levels. By spurring markets for innovative technologies, preventing pollution, and reducing the deficit, this initiative could save taxpayers $1 billion annually in reduced energy bills.

The four Federal agencies that consume the vast majority of energy, the Departments of Defense, Energy, and Veterans Affairs and the General Services Administration, had increased funding for energy efficiency measures in their budgets by more than 60% for 1994, four times greater than 1993.

A 1994 survey by the Association of Energy Engineers (Atlanta, GA) found that 23.3% of members saw $100,000 to $500,000 in savings from installed energy management technologies, while 13.8% saw $500,000 to $1 million in cost savings.

The U.S. Environmental Protection Agency introduced a new program in 1994 which follows the *Green Lights, Energy Star, and VISITT* programs. The *Building Air Quality Alliance* is aimed at indoor air quality and will stimulate voluntary standards and allow the private sector to regulate itself. EPA's Office of Radiation and Indoor Air feels that, regarding IAQ, the highly selected environment does not lend itself well to a regulatory approach. Inspection of individual buildings represents prohibitive cost, not to mention the possible infringement of privacy.

There were numerous major energy conservation projects initiated and/or implemented throughout 1994. Following is a sampling of projects reported by *Energy User News*:

- A retrofit of 5,460 windows was completed in June 1994 at the Empire state building at a cost of $5.5 million; annual energy savings are estimated to be $948,000. There were no utility rebates.

- Ft. Polk Army Base (Louisiana) initiated an $18 million project in September 1994 to retrofit 4,000 housing units with efficient ground-source heat pumps and implementing other HVAC, lighting, and building envelope upgrades.

- A comprehensive lighting retrofit was completed in Kearney (Calif.) High School in November 1994 at a cost of $160,187; the project will serve as a model for retrofits in 160 more schools. San Diego Gas & Electric awarded a $25,599 rebate.

- The Federal Reserve Bank initiated a $300,000 retrofit that included the installation of high-efficiency motors and variable frequency drives. Annual savings of 1.4 MMkWh/yr. are expected. The projects was completely paid for by Boston Edison.

- MGM Grand Hotel (Las Vegas, NV) installed seven 1,750 kW diesel engines at a cost of $2.5 million. The powerplant will provide emergency power to keep slot machines operating in the event of a power failure, and reduce its summer demand charges by $434,880 by allowing the facility to participate in Nevada Power Company's peak shaving program.

- In June 1994, the Jersey City Public School District (Jersey City, NJ) began a 24-school lighting retrofit to reduce electricity demand by 1.7 megawatts and generate an annual net positive cashflow of $306,824. The district-wide relamping cost approximately $1,819,000. which will be paid by Public Service Conservation Resources Corporation (Parsippany, NJ), an unregulated subsidiary of the district's utility, Public Service Electric and Gas.

- The State of Washington's Department of Ecology (Lacey, WA) built a new energy-efficient headquarters in 1994 that is expected to reduce the building's annual energy consumption 30%. In total, the efficiency improvements are expected to save the building 2,309,446 kilowatt hours per year. The $732,878 incremental cost of the energy-conscious upgrades was offset by $507,862 in rebates from the local utility, Puget Power and Light, leaving a net incremental cost of $225,016. The rebate accelerated the project's payback by 5.5 years, to 2.4 years, based on expected annual utility bill savings of $92,379.

- AT&T Bell Laboratories Indian Hills Complex (Naperville, IL) is expected to save approximately 15 million kilowatt hours and $1.2 million per year due to a 15,000 point building automation system that uses spare points on variable air volume controllers to provide lighting control. In June 1993, a Metasys direct digital control building automation system by Johnson Controls, Inc. (Milwaukee, WI), was installed in the 1.2 million square foot main building of the complex. The Metasys installation and ventilation system upgrade cost approximately $3.5 million. Based on expected electricity bill savings, payback will occur in just under three years.

- The Marine Corps Base Camp Pendleton (Oceanside, CA) completed a 280-building lighting retrofit in September 1994. San Diego Gas & Electric Company provided a rebate and loan assistance for the $1.3 million undertaking that covered three million square feet. The utility provided a $500,000 rebate and arranged four bank loans to finance the $800,000 balance.

- In September 1994, General American Life Insurance Company's National Service Center (St. Louis, MO) completed a multiphase retrofit to lower utility costs and enhance indoor air quality. Electricity consumption is expected to decrease by over 11 million kilowatt hours annually, lowering operating costs by $1.68 per square foot. The $2.4 million effort will save $419,993 in annual power bills.

- In December 1993, Hughes Space and Communications Company (Los Angeles, CA) completed an eight-building lighting retrofit that is expected to save $752,461 annually in electricity bills and reduce consumption by 1,141 kilowatts per year.

Southern California Edison Company's Energy Management Hardware Rebate Program provided a $217,625 rebate.

- Boston Edison agreed to pay the entire $1,251,623 cost of on-going energy-efficiency upgrades at the Thomas P. O'Neill, Jr. federal building (Boston, MA). The first phase of the U.S. General Services Administration project, a $1,026,648 lighting upgrade, was completed in July 1994. The second phase will cost $224,975 and be completed in early 1995.

- St. Charles Medical Center initiated a performance-contract-backed energy conservation retrofit that is guaranteed to reduce the facility's electricity usage by 3,434,167 kilowatt hours. The $2,333,875 project, completed in December 1994, is expected to cut annual utility and maintenance costs by $276,826. The retrofit is expected to reduce the five-building, 330,000 square foot hospital's year gas usage by 18,111 million Btu. Rebates totalling $615,000 were awarded by Central Electric Cooperative, Inc. (Redmond, OR). Payback is expected in 6.2 years.

- In January 1994, Toyota Auto Body of California, Inc. (Long Beach, CA) installed new variable-speed drives on industrial process motors. This is expected to cut the factory's annual electricity consumption by 47%, or 2,118,933 kilowatt hours. The project cost $988,683. The drives alone accounted for $300,000 of the expense and resulted in a $63,568 rebate from Southern California Edison Company under its Energy Management Hardware Program. Annual utility cost savings are expected to be $158,024, which will yield a payback of 5.85 years.

- In December 1993, Barry University (Miami Shores, FL) completed a campus-wide lighting retrofit that is expected to save 2.72 million kilowatt hours annually and reduce the school's demand by 620 kilowatts. The project was conducted under a performance contract with energy service company ConServ Energy Technologies, Inc. (Boca Raton, FL), a subsidiary of Eastern Utilities (Boston, MA). Annual utility cost savings attributable to the retrofit are expected to total $300,000.

- In January 1994, Southern California Edison awarded California State University (Fullerton) a rebate totalling more than $1 million. The university installed new energy-efficient equipment to earn one of the largest rebates ever given by the utility. CSUF upgraded its heating and cooling plant to all-electric facilities, upgraded lighting, installed a thermal energy storage systems, and made other efficiency improvements, in order to reduce usage by 7.9 million kWh annually, at yearly savings of $600,000.

There were also some exciting trade shows in 1994. *Power-Gen*, just five years old, joined the ranks of the 200 largest shows in the U.S., according to Tradeshow Week

(Los Angeles). The 1994 Power-Gen conference, held December 1994 in Orlando, attracted about 14,000 attendees. The ninth annual *Competitive Power Congress*, June 1994 in Philadelphia, sponsored by the Association of Energy Engineers, was noticeably larger and more heavily attended than in previous years. The World Energy Engineering Congress, in its 16th year and the premier energy management trade show, was held in Atlanta, December 1994, in conjunction with the *Environmental Technology Expo* and the *Plant and Facilities Expo*. The annual *International Air-Conditioning, Heating, and Refrigeration Expo*, sponsored by ASHRAE, was held in New Orleans in January 1994, and saw the introduction of new energy-efficient HVAC, controls products and refrigerant management equipment, however, four of the top five cooling equipment vendors did not exhibit -- Carrier Corporation (Syracuse, NY), SnyderGeneral Corporation (Dallas, TX), The Trane Company (LaCrosse, WI) and York International Corporation (York, PA). At *LightFair*, held in New York May 1994, approximately 14,000 attendees saw an emphasis on energy-related themes.

10.3 Short Term Outlook

The slowing of demand-side management rebates by electric utilities is expected to begin to hurting the energy management business in 1995. Some vendors of energy-saving equipment are worried that customers have gotten so addicted to rebate programs that they may not buy anything without them. In a recent issue of *Energy User News*, the president of an occupancy sensor company said, "Large rebates will prove to be a deterrent to the conservation effort in the long run. To customers used to receiving large rebates for energy-efficient products, these products will seem high-priced once utilities stop paying for them."

The effects of DSM cut-backs will be localized, as only certain utility programs have reduced their rebates. Others are still committed to existing programs and rebate reductions may occur in the future. This may actually spur some users to implement their energy reduction measures now while rebates are still available. Specific energy conservation products expected to be impacted the most will be those which are most favored in rebate programs (see data in section 9.1 of this report).

Federal energy management should be even stronger in 1995. The 1995 budget will implement provisions contained in EPAct that allow agencies to retain 50% of their energy efficiency savings and rebates. This will provide a powerful incentive for agencies to seek additional energy and money saving opportunities.

Standards on indoor air quality (IAQ) may be promulgated as part of OSHA reform or as separate standards. Already an important issue in energy engineering and HVAC, IAQ now has only customer interests and potential liabilities as a market driver. Legislation would definitely bring IAQ to the forefront.

The laws are fully in place to phase out manufacturing of CFC-based refrigerants by the end of 1995. The risks facing building owners and managers are very real. Non-compliance or poor refrigerant transitional planning can cost many thousands of dollars in crisis management. While most majority of industries had addressed the CFC issue, there will still be a lot of activity as companies face the deadline in 1995.

10.4 Mid-Range and Long Term Outlook

Despite some possible temporary slow-down in energy conservation spending if utility rebate programs slow down, the energy management field will stay strong for the next decade because of the potential cost savings which can be achieved by the industrial, commercial, federal, and residential sectors.

Large energy reduction measures are expected to occur in the industrial sector, particularly if higher energy costs provide new incentives. The U.S. Department of Energy has estimated the technical and achievable industrial energy-savings potentials in 2010 are 27% and 13%, respectively. The U.S. Congress' Office of Technology Assessment estimates the potential industrial energy savings in 2015 as between 11% to 37%. Several other studies estimate the electricity savings potential in the industrial sector as between 9% to 38%. The Electric Power Research Institute estimates the maximum technical electricity savings potential in the industrial sector is between 24% and 38% in 2000, relative to a business-as-usual scenario. The biggest opportunity for improvement lies in motor drives, which account for 67% of the industrial electricity used today. Essentially, motors keep American industry moving, operating fans, blowers, pumps, compressors, blenders, conveyors, and process lines. To take advantage of the full potential for savings, industries would be using high-efficiency motors with adjustable-speed drives (ASDs) that allow for efficient and smooth variations in motor speed. Work areas would be illuminated with efficient lighting systems that incorporate high-frequency ballasts, improved reflective fixtures, and sophisticated lighting controls similar to those in the commercial sector.

In the commercial sector, anywhere between 23% and 49% of the electricity projected to be used in 2000 could be saved. The biggest contributors for potential savings are lighting, space cooling, and various "plug loads," such as office equipment, computers, and copy machines. An ongoing EPRI project has shown that much electricity can be saved in commercial buildings through the integrated design of heating, ventilating, and air conditioning systems with lighting systems. Results indicate that if more-efficient strategies were applied to only 5% of existing U.S. commercial spaces and to 25% of new construction each year, they could save 1,400 MW annually, the equivalent output of one and a half large power plants. These better designs would dramatically reduce peak loads for utilities, particularly during the summer, when air conditioning systems create substantial demand.

By the year 2000, EPA's Green Lights goal is to have 24 billion to 60 billion square feet committed. At the end of 1992, Green Lights had 2.9 billion square feet, or about 3% of all commercial/industrial space.

In the residential sector, anywhere between 27% and 46% of the electricity used in 2000 could be saved. The biggest contributors to the potential savings are technological advancements in water heating, space heating, and miscellaneous appliances, of which lighting represents 45%. To achieve this level of efficiency, homes would be weatherstripped and caulked, have storm windows and doors, and ceilings and floors would be well insulated. Efficient electric heat pumps and solar panels would reduce energy use for space and water heating. Compact fluorescent bulbs with incandescent-like color spectrums would light lamps. Among the biggest energy savers available for homes today is the electric heat pump.

EPRI's studies show that electric utilities project an 8.5% improvement in energy efficiency by 2000, due to new federal and state efficiency standards and market response to higher energy prices. Another study co-sponsored with the Edison Electric Institute reports that utility-sponsored programs in demand-side management will reduce summer peak demand by 6.7% or 45 GW.

According to a feature in *Electric Light & Power* (July 1994), cost-effective, large-scale uses of high-temperature superconductors are imminent within three to six years. Impending commercial applications include: 1,000 horsepower motors, with half the losses of existing high-efficiency motors, for about the same cost; 50 kilowatthours (kWh) of kinetic energy stored in floating flywheels to help meet daily peaks, comparable in cost to combustion turbines; and electricity storage devices for 0.5 MWh to 20 MWh that can automatically discharge to stabilize a grid.

It is virtually certain that natural gas cooling techniques and energy sources (such as absorption cooling, desiccant dehumidification, and fuel cells) will assume a larger role in air conditioning in the coming decades. Gas cooling reduces energy costs, and depending upon the system configuration, reduce or eliminate the use of CFCs.

10.5 Opportunities

With diminishing utility rebates for energy conservation, Energy Savings Performance Contracting, also known as Shared Energy Savings Contracting, will gain in popularity as an alternative to traditional methods of financing energy efficiency improvements. Under this alternative financing arrangement, companies or federal agencies contract with energy-service companies, who pay all the up-front costs. These costs include identifying building energy requirements and acquiring, installing, operating, and maintaining the energy-efficient equipment. In exchange, the contractor receives a share of the cost savings resulting from these improvements until the contract period expires, which can be up to 25 years. At that time, the company or federal government retains all the savings and equipment.

11 POWER GENERATION CONSTRUCTION AND EQUIPMENT

CONTENTS:

11.1 Trends and Market Assessment
11.2 Recent Activities
11.3 Short Term Outlook
11.4 Mid-Range and Long Term Outlook
11.5 Opportunities

11.1 Trends and Market Assessment

Overall spending on construction by both industry and utilities has been increasing in recent years. Electric utility construction makes up more than 10% of the U.S. construction industry.

According to the U.S. Department of Commerce, several segments of the electric power construction market that prospered even during the economic slump of the early 1990s continued to do well through the mid-1990s, including transmission facilities, retrofits of existing power plants, and pollution control systems. Retrofits to improve the efficiency and extend the generating life of power plants involve much less risk and require fewer permits than "greenfield" construction at new sites. Utilities will continue to invest heavily in transmission systems to accommodate growth and make optimum use of existing power plants. Pollution control spending will increase because of tightening environmental restrictions and a federal government program to subsidize clean coal technology. Expenditures for the maintenance and repair of electric utility systems have grown rapidly and are almost as large as new utility construction spending. Maintenance and repair expenditures will continue to grow rapidly in the 1990s, as the average age of operating power plants increases and as operations become more complex.

Non-utility generators are investing, in part, instead of electric utilities, for additional generating capacity. The growth in demand is projected by the utilities to increase at only 1.5% per year.

11.2 Recent Activities

According to a preliminary estimate by the Edison Electric Institute, investor-owned utility construction expenditures were $25.90 billion in 1994, and distributed as follows (change from 1993 in parenthesis):

- Coal-fired plants: $4.32 billion (+4.3%)
- Nuclear generating plants: $2.67 billion (+7.2%)
- Other generation types: $2.45 billion (+150.7%)
- Transmission facilities: $2.70 billion (+1.3%)
- Distribution facilities: $8.64 billion (-3.4%)
- Other: $5.12 billion

While 1994 expenditures were slightly more than in 1993, they were below the level which had been planned, reflecting IOU's efforts to reduce the capital intensity of generation to be more competitive.

Based on a survey of more than 100 utilities (municipals, cooperatives, federal, and investor-owned), representing approximately 65% of U.S. generating capacity, *Electric Light and Power* (January 1994) projects U.S. electric utility capital spending as follows:

- 1992: $26.5 billion
- 1993: $29.7 billion
- 1994: $31.8 billion
- 1995: $31.8 billion
- 1996: $26.3 billion
- 1997: $27.3 billion

Projected spending for future years probably reflects a lack of reporting rather than an actual decline.

The distribution of projected 1994 capital spending, and change from 1993 are:

- Generation: $8.9 billion, +15%
- Distribution: $8.3 billion, +6%
- Transmission: $3.5 billion, -1%
- Air pollution control: $2.7 billion, +20%
- Substation: $1.3 billion, -4%
- DSM/load management: $1.0 billion, +17%
- Other: $6.1 billion, -4%

According to JTB Associates (San Diego, CA), 8,640 MW of generating capacity were commissioned in 1994, distributed as follows:

- Natural gas and oil: 7,400 MW
- Coal and other fossil: 460 MW
- Renewables: 780 MW

Expenditures for maintenance and repair of electric utility systems have grown rapidly and are almost as large as new construction expenditures. These expenditures will continue to grow rapidly in the 1990s, as the average use of operating power plants increase and operations become more complex.

An annual survey of worldwide gas turbine orders is conducted annually by *Diesel & Gas Turbine Worldwide*. The 1994 report showed strong growth. Total worldwide orders increased to 796 (27 MW) for June 1993 to May 1994 from 656 orders (25,590 MW) in the previous twelve month period. North America accounted for 162 of the orders. The Far East led the market with 216 orders, followed by Western Europe with 173.

Orders for diesel, gas and dual-fuel engines increased to 4,021 (8,388 MW) for June 1993 to May 1994 from 3,028 (7,107 MW) during the previous twelve months. North America led the market with 901 orders.

According to CRS Market Data Sources (Tulsa, OK), utility spending plans for generating plant control systems declined slightly in 1994, but remain at a fairly high level. A CRS survey found 400 control system projects valued at $547 million planned or under way for the 30-month period between October 1994 and April 1997.

According to The Freedonia Group (Cleveland, OH), the 1994 U.S. electric power equipment market was:

- Electric power equipment demand: $9.9 billion

- Electric power equipment shipments: $9.8 billion
  - Transformers: $3.4 billion
  - Switchgear: $5.9 billion
  - Pole & transmission hardware: $0.56 billion

Several major independent power generation announcements were made in 1994. They are discussed in the following paragraphs.

Sacramento Municipal Utility District announced in September 1994 agreements to purchase power from four new cogeneration plants which would be completed from 2000 to 2008. Owners are Carson Energy Group, Campbell Soup Company, Proctor & Gamble, and ARK Energy, Inc.

Also in September, CRSS, Inc. (Houston, TX) and Phillips Coal Company (Dallas, TX) announced plans to build a $600 million lignite-burning powerplant in northeast Mississippi with a capacity of 300 MW to 400 MW. It will be the first new generating station built in the state since the early 1980s and its first IPP.

The Colville Confederated Tribes announced in early-1994 that they would build a 400-MW gas-fired cogeneration plant themselves in eastern Washington. A consultant is to be hired, and project plans are expected to be completed by the end of 1997. The tribe had been negotiating with Mission Energy (Irvine, CA) and Unocol Corporation (Los Angeles).

In early 1994, Btu Energy, Inc. (Bellevue, WA) and Siemens Power Ventures (New York, NY) announced plans for a $450 million, 438 MW gas-fired power plant in Montana for Columbia Falls Aluminum Company The move is one of several efforts by various parties to free themselves from dependence on Bonneville Power Administration, which raised rates 15.7% in October 1993 and likely has more hikes ahead. Opposition is anticipated from the new Energy Facility Siting Council.

In another effort to reduce dependence on Bonneville Power Administration, Clark County, WA announced in April 1994 that Cogentrix Energy, Inc. (Charlotte, NC) would build for them a 240 MW gas-fired plant.

In September 1994, Portland General Electric announced a 440 MW gas-fired combustion turbine power plant. Building new utility-owned plants in the Far West is fairly rare. PGE received about 50 unsolicited proposals for a total of 5,000 MW from IPPs but decided that it could replace capacity at less cost itself. Construction will be by Raytheon Constructors. The new Coyote Springs plant will make up for some of the capacity lost when PGE closed the only nuclear unit in Oregon, the 1,100 MW Trojan plant.

11.3 Short Term Outlook

The Edison Electric Institute forecasts that investor-owned utility construction expenditures will be $24.91 billion in 1995, a decrease of 3.8% from 1994. The decrease is due to utility cost reduction measures, and would be even greater except for the intermediate lead time between commitment and expenditures. The distribution of 1995 expenditures is forecast to be (change from 1993 in parenthesis):

- Coal-fired plants: $3.63 billion (-16.0%)
- Nuclear generating plants: $2.12 billion (-20.6%)
- Other generation types: $3.66 billion (+24.0%)
- Transmission facilities: $2.89 billion (+6.9%)
- Distribution facilities: $8.83 billion (+1.1%)

According to CRS Market Data Services (Tulsa, OK), electric utilities in the United States and Canada are planning 648 power plant maintenance outages between October 1994 and April 1997, valued at more than $1 billion. The value of the 1995 outages is approximately $400 million.

CRS Market Data Services forecasts U.S. and Canadian utilities will spend $567.6

million on 402 supervisory control and data acquisition/energy management system (SCADA/EMS) projects during the 30-month period from June 1994 to January 1997. The 1995 value is approximately $225 million.

11.4 Mid-Range and Long Term Outlook

According to Mick Linn of PSI Energy, Inc. and chairman of the Edison Electric Institute construction committee, there should be major increases in generating construction in the near future that will add up to about $76 billion of expenditures between 1994 and 2002. This new capacity will be different from construction of the past. Estimates of the non-utility portion of new generation range up to 20,000 MW. New utility generating projects will have to be justifiable in terms of integrated resource planning.

Construction expenditures by investor-owned utilities will again decrease in 1996, according to the Edison Electric Institute. Total expenditures of $24.23 billion are forecast, distributed as follows:

- Coal-fired plants: $3.68 billion
- Nuclear generating plants: $1.88 billion
- Other generation types: $2.94 billion
- Transmission facilities: $2.92 billion
- Distribution facilities: $8.95 billion

Significant need for additional baseload capacity will begin around the middle of the next decade, according to the U.S. Department of Energy. Demand for electricity in the United States is expected to grow and 200 gigawatts of new generating capacity will be needed by 2010, according to the Department of Energy's (DoE) Pittsburgh Energy

Technology Center (PETC).

Gas turbines are expected to be used to meet much of this new demand. Today's turbines will fulfill only a portion of this needed capacity; new ones will be needed for the rest. Several programs are under way to develop these needed new combustion turbines, in particular those sponsored by PETC and DoE's Morgantown Energy Technology Center.

According to The Freedonia Group, Inc. (Cleveland, OH), U.S. demand for electric power equipment will increase 4.8%, reaching $11.9 billion in 1998. Electric power equipment shipments by U.S. manufacturers are forecast to be $111.7 billion in 1998 (average 1993-98 growth rates given in parenthesis):

- Transformers: $4.1 billion (4.9%)
- Switchgear: $7.0 billion (4.6%)
- Pole and transmission hardware: $0.6 billion (1.8%)

Market growth will be the result of moderate increases in electricity consumption, investment by electric utilities and housing starts, and strong expansion of industrial activity and industrial plant and equipment investment. The electric power equipment market will see minimal price increases because the industry is a mature business both in terms of market saturation and technology (these manufacturing processes are well known and easy to replicate). Three primary trends are influencing the transformer market, which will exceed $4 billion in 1998. Among these, changes in electric utility regulation and electricity pricing are causing industrial users to increase their bulk purchases of electricity and step up cogeneration of electricity. As a result, the market for power transformers is shifting away from electric utilities to industrial customers.

Another trend involves a shift in the market from pole-mounted to pad-mounted distribution transformers as new housing and small commercial facilities are increasingly supplied by underground electrical systems. Finally, the rapid expansion of the industrial equipment transformer market is making voltage regulating transformers more important. This growth is the result of the increased use of more sensitive electrical equipment (e.g., computers), which makes fluctuations in electric current more costly and necessitates the use of equipment to control the power supply. The switchgear market is expected to reach $7 billion in 1998, driven by two primary influences. First, the increasing penetration of electrical equipment and processes into industry, coupled with expanding investment in industrial equipment, is accelerating demand for switchgear by manufacturing sectors. Secondly, electronic-based switching equipment is multifunctional and can be easily connected to a communications system and controlled remotely, which means fewer people can monitor entire systems and faults can be more efficiently isolated and found. Utilities are expected to rely more heavily on this type of system as they attempt to cut costs. Also, as industrial electrical systems become more complex, manufacturers will use more electronic switchgear. Despite these developments, the U.S. electric power equipment market is mature. In order to expand markets, firms are looking overseas, particularly to Southeast Asia and Latin America. Overseas markets pose two major barriers: 1) most countries' electric utilities are run by the government and favor local suppliers, and 2) large amounts of capital and complete product lines are needed to compete internationally. However, the former barrier is changing as many countries privatize their utilities.

Of the total energy capacity added in the United States between 1993 and 2010, 53% is expected to be gas turbine combined cycle and combustion turbine plants.

Several major projects in the United States are scheduled for completion in the near future.

Quadrex Corporation and the Seminole Indian Tribe of Florida, Inc. are conducting a feasibility study that could lead to the development of a $2 billion, 2,000 MW independent powerplant on the Brighton Indian Reservation, northwest of Lake Okeechobee in south central Florida. The plant is expected to have three to five generating units. Bechtel Power Corporation (Gaithersburg, MD) is providing technical support.

A 3,000 MW gas fired plant is under construction by Florida Power. The $3 billion plant will be built five miles northwest of Fort Meade and completed by 2001.

A joint venture of Black & Veatch Power Development Corporation and NRG Energy, an affiliate of Northern States Power Company, will build the country's largest independent power plant near Okeechobee, FL. The 800 MW plant will have two coal-fired units and cost more than $1 billion. The units will have the most advanced air pollution control equipment and the design will not require potable water for cooling. The plant will tap an aquifer that produces water too brackish for drinking. Construction will be complete in 1997.

Tampa Electric Company is building a 1,000 MW coal gasification plant south of Mulberry in Polk County (Florida). The $1 billion power plant is scheduled for completion in 2001.

11.5 Opportunities

There are good construction and equipment opportunities in the United States for repowering. A study by the Gas Research Institute on the potential for repowering in U.S. electric utilities found it could add up to 151 GW of capacity during the next 20 years. The study indicates the need for capacity additions coincides with a time period when a large percentage of fossil generating units will show the accelerating effects of aging. It concludes that a surge in repowering activity should be expected during the next decade because these factors coincide. Thirty units, comprising three GW of capacity have been proposed for repowering. In addition, the study projects that as repowering activity accelerates, the typical size of a project will increase. Current repowering is being done and planned for 1950s-vintage fossil plants. As technology advanced, larger and larger units were built, starting in the 1950s and continuing through the early 1970s. Consequently, the older units typically are much smaller and simpler than the national average. It further notes that the output rating of the average coal steam unit is 13% below its nameplate capability, and current repowering plans will recapture 96% of this loss.

Repowering is the integration of modern technology into an existing powerplant site. It increases the available capacity at the site, which increases the heat rate efficiency, lowers emissions at the site, and eliminates as much as 50% of the cost associated with greenfield development of new powerplants. Repowering of existing utility power plants represents one of the largest potential development opportunities over the next 12 to 15 years for both utilities and non-utility generators. DoE has estimated that, as of 1991, approximately 2,500 utility generating plants were 30 years old or older. This number will increase to between 3,500 and 3,700 by 1998.

12 TRANSMISSION AND DISTRIBUTION

CONTENTS:

12.1 Trends and Market Assessment
12.2 Recent Activities
12.3 Short Term Outlook
12.4 Mid-Range and Long Term Outlook
12.5 Opportunities

12.1 Trends and Market Assessment

According to *Electric Light & Power* (January 1994) capital spending by U.S.

utilities for transmission is:

- 1992 (actual): $3.0 billion
- 1993 (estimated): $3.5 billion
- 1994 (projected): $3.5 billion
- 1995 (projected): $3.7 billion
- 1996 (projected): $2.9 billion
- 1997 (projected): $3.2 billion

Capital spending for distribution is:

- 1992 (actual): $6.7 billion
- 1993 (estimated): $7.8 billion
- 1994 (projected): $8.3 billion
- 1995 (projected): $8.5 billion
- 1996 (projected): $7.6 billion
- 1997 (projected): $7.8 billion

Projected expenditures may be low because of a lack of reporting in the *EL&P* survey rather than an actual decline.

According to a 1994 survey of 65 public power systems by Resource Management International (Austin, TX), significant changes have evolved in underground residential distribution (URD) since 1990. The predominant voltage class continues to be 15 kilovolts. In addition, 14 systems report they are uprating their systems to 15 kV. Just four reported predominant use of 25 kV and only one utility reported predominant use of 35 kV primary. There is a trend away from direct burial and toward cable installed in conduit systems, with 75% of the respondents using conduit for residential customers. This is up from 60% in 1990.

12.2 Recent Activities

1994 saw the recognition of comparability as a basis for transmission pricing by the Federal Energy Regulatory Commission. In a case involving American Electric Power Company, FERC stated that a transmission owner should charge itself on the same or comparable basis that it charges others for the same service. FERC said that it would apply five principles in judging whether individual filings meet the requirements of the Federal Power Act:

- Traditional revenue requirements
- Comparability
- promptness of economic efficiency
- Fairness
- Practicality

According to the Edison Electric Institute, investor owned expenditures for transmission system construction were $2.7 billion in 1994. This amount is down sharply from the $3.3 billion to $4.0 billion which had been previously planned for the year, and less than earlier years through 1989.

Investor-owned utilities spent less on distribution in 1994 than in the four previous years. According to the Edison Electric Institute, the 1994 expenditure was $8.64 billion, a decrease of 3.4% from 1993.

At the October 1994 Applied Superconductivity Conference (Boston), American Superconductor Corporation (Boston, MA) unveiled a proposed prototype high-temperature superconductor (HTS) power cable designed to carry between 2,000 amps and 3,000 amps at 77K. EPRI contends that HTS cables can be a cost-effective alternative to copper cable for many new and retrofit applications.

There are indications that electric utilities are becoming more receptive to offering transmission access to independent power producers. The 1994 Cogeneration/IPP Production Survey by the Association of Energy Engineers (Atlanta, GA) asked "what is the transmission access environment in 1994 as compared to 1993?" Responses were:

- Utilities more responsive: 30%
- Utilities less responsive: 13%
- Same: 57%

According to the U.S. Department of Commerce, the 1994 market for transformers was $3.3 billion (1987 constant dollars). Demand for power and distribution transformers comes primarily from expansion and maintenance in the electric utility industry. Sales of distribution transformers depend primarily on new housing starts. Other market factors include voltage conversions, upgrading of small voltage units, equipment failures, conversions to more efficient units in response to higher energy costs, and kilowatt hour (kWh) sales growth. The depressed residential construction market, and a more energy-conscious consumer have reduced the demand for distribution transformers in recent years, however, the rejuvenation of the residential construction market will help to stimulate the demand of these padmount transformers. The primary domestic consumers of liquid-immersed distribution transformers are investor-owned utilities, accounting for close to 70% of the unit demand of this type of transformer. Municipal utilities and industrial plants make up the rest of the market. In the unregulated IPP environment, imported transformers dominate the highly competitive international market. This combination of factors could overshadow what may at first appear to be a positive sign for the overall transformer industry. Shipments of transformers are expected to increase less than 3% in 1994 with the rebounding U.S. economy.

According to the U.S. Department of Commerce, the 1994 market for switchgear products was $4.57 billion (1987 constant dollars). Switchgear products include switches, fuses, panelboards, distribution boards, and circuit breakers. These products are used primarily in generation, transmission, and distribution systems. They are required for load switching, short circuit protection, and in industrial and commercial power systems for protecting and controlling circuit loads. The market increased by approximately 3% in 1994.

12.3 Short Term Outlook

Utilities are reluctant to construct new transmission facilities other than urgently needed lines and substations. The Edison Electric Institute forecasts that transmission system capital expenditures by IOUs will be $2.89 billion in 1995, an increase of 6.9% from 1994, but still significantly less than the pre-1989 era.

Expenditures for distribution system construction will be less in 1995 than previously planned for the year, and also less than previous years. An expenditure of $8.83 billion is forecast by the Edison Electric Institute.

New Jersey's Board of Public Utilities will investigate whether utilities should separate their transmission business from generation in 1995, as part of Phase II of a master plan to open supply of new electric capacity to competition.

12.4 Mid-Range and Long Term Outlook

The low expected growth rate in demand and uncertainty of cost recovery in the pricing in competitive, open-access era will limit new transmission construction by IOUs. The Edison Electric Institute forecasts expenditures of $2.92 billion in 1996.

Utilities will continue to spend less on distribution according to the Edison Electric Institute. An expenditure of $8.95 billion is forecast for 1996. This amount is only $12 million more than spent in 1993, and after correcting for inflation, real spending is not increasing.

According to a survey by the Washington International Energy Group (Washington, DC), 67% of respondents reported their companies plan to start adding transmission capacity after the year 2000. However, in a previous survey, 42% of respondents indicated they were already building new transmission capacity, and 40% expected to add new transmission capacity within five years.

High-temperature superconductor materials have the potential of revolutionizing the distribution of electricity in the future. EPRI estimates that some 2,200 miles of existing cables in the U.S. are candidates for replacement with HTS cables. About 20% of the underground transmission cables in the U.S. are nearing the end of their planned 30 to 40 year design life and may require replacement through 2005.

According to Arthur Andersen & Company (New York, NY) and Cambridge Energy Research Associates, Inc. (Cambridge, MA), power distribution is one area where the traditional approach to utility regulation, rate-based capital investments, monopoly territorial franchises, and revenue requirement budgeting, could carry forward into the 21st century. Opportunities for strategic success will largely depend on the evolution of the regulatory framework and the ability of utilities to adapt to both changing regulatory requirements and increasingly sophisticated customer needs. For utilities that are most responsive to change and understand the needs of newly defined customer classes (some for "ultra-clean" power, for example), making money the old-fashioned way may be a realistic and rewarding objective.

A new high-voltage transmission system is being planned for the southeast, from Alabama to South Florida. The estimated cost is about $500 million. Two Florida utilities will pay to build, operate, and maintain the new transmission section. The transmission line will run a total of 480 miles.

Increased levels of electric utility and non-residential construction (particularly industrial construction) activity will sustain the demand for switchgear products in the future. Growth in demand for switchgear products is forecast to grow at an annual rate of 3% to 4% between 1994 and 1998.

12.5 Opportunities

According to Mason Willrich, president and CEO of PG&E Enterprises (San Francisco, CA), future electric utilities will be more like distribution and transmission companies and less like generation companies. To this end, electric utilities will modernize their distribution systems. At the customer level, utilities are expected to replace their existing meters with ones that can be read remotely. These meters would also have the capability of remotely controlling a customer's appliances.

By retrofitting existing underground transmission systems with high temperature superconducting cables, utilities could increase power transmission of their systems 50% to 500%.

13 FOSSIL FUEL GENERATION

CONTENTS:

13.1 Trends and Market Assessment
13.2 Recent Activities
13.3 Short Term Outlook
13.4 Mid-Range and Long Term Outlook
13.5 Opportunities

13.1 Trends and Market Assessment

According to the U.S. Energy Information Administration, U.S. expenditures on coal energy were $21.0 billion in 1993. More than three-quarters of U.S. coal production is sold to electric utilities, where it generates more than half of the electric power in the U.S. An additional 10% or 11% of U.S. coal, on average, is exported.

The coal industry must contend, directly or indirectly, with some of the most difficult environmental issues in U.S. industry. Some of these issues, including land reclamation and the health of miners, have been dealt with through the mechanism of trust funds, funded through excise taxes levied on coal production. Other environmental issues, including the consequences of emissions of coal-fired power plants, have been more difficult to improve.

Although 41 coal plants have been ordered since 1979, 58 have been cancelled during the same period. Market forces, influenced by regulatory, environmental and legislative factors, have paralyzed utilities which no longer have any confidence that new plants can be placed into the rate base with an acceptable rate of return on investment.

The Department of Energy's Clean Coal Technology Program has seen an investment of $2.4 billion by the federal government and almost $4.6 billion by the private sector since its inception in 1985. The program is aimed at enabling the nation to use its plentiful domestic coal resources to provide clean, coal-based power and still meet environmental quality requirements. At the end of 1993, 23 projects were either in operation or had completed their test runs.

Over the last 20 years, the addition of coal-fired power plants in the United States has eroded from a market of 10 GW to 15 GW annually to approximately 1 GW in 1992. The loss of marketshare is partially a result of higher capital costs of coal-fired power plants facing increasingly stringent environmental requirements compared to the lower costs of other power generating options.

Natural gas generates 9.5% of U.S. electric power, and utilities use 14.9% of U.S. natural gas consumption.

13.2 Recent Activities

In March 1994, the Energy Information Administration released its statistics on 1993 power generation by utilities. Total net generation in the United States was 2,882,212 gigawatts, distributed as follows (change from 1992 in parenthesis):

- Coal: 56.9% (+4%)
- Nuclear: 21.2% (-1%)

- Hydroelectric: 9.2% (+11%)
- Natural gas: 9.0% (-2%)
- Oil: 3.5% (+12%)
- Other: 0.3% (-6%)

The 1993 generation was about 3% higher than in the previous year. Coal, oil and hydroelectric generation met the higher demand caused primarily by weather and, to a lesser degree from economic growth.

According to JTB & Associates (San Diego, CA), in 1994, three coal or culm plants commissioned for a total of 460 MW.

According to the Energy Information Administration (EIA) of the U.S. Department of Energy, natural gas demand associated with increased output of electricity by electric utilities and industrial cogenerators accounts for the bulk of the nearly 1.2 trillion cubic feet of increased natural gas use (under base conditions) for the 1993 to 1995 period. In 1994, utility gas demand rose by 8.0%. Demand for gas by nonutility generators increased at a rate of 9.6% in 1994.

Total coal consumption increased by 2.2% in 1994. Growth in electricity demand was the only major source of growth in coal demand. Coal production increased a total of almost 80 million tons in 1994.

The American Gas Association's (AGA) 1994 Mid-Year Base Case projected U.S. natural gas consumption at 21.6 quads (quadrillion Btus) for the year. AGA attributed this high usage to strong economic growth and rising oil prices. This would be the highest level of natural gas consumption since 1973 and a 4% increase over 1993. The association also predicted the seven year trend of rising gas consumption, begun in

1987, would continue in 1994.

Natural gas use in the electric industry was predicted to rise by 0.2 quads in 1994 compared to 1993, a 6% increase. According to AGA, gas use in the industry depended on demand for electricity, oil and coal prices, and availability of nuclear and hydroelectric power.

A 1994 report by Utility Data Institute (Washington, DC) concluded that the least-cost producers of electricity in the United States over the five-year period 1989 to 1993 are coal-fired power plants west of the Mississippi River burning low-sulfur coal. The analysis, published in *U.S. Steam-Electric Plants: Five-Year Production Costs*, is based on an analysis of 707 power plants producing 85% of U.S. electric utility output. These power plants spent $267 billion for operations, maintenance and fuel during the five-year period. A breakdown of the 707 facilities is: 402 coal-fired plants, 173 gas-fired plants, 55 oil-fired plants, 66 nuclear power plants, and 11 plants burning other fuels.

A panel at the 1994 Gas Mart conference (Chicago) discussed the impact of power market deregulation on the gas industry. The panel concluded that the interaction between natural gas and electric generation will be even greater as the power market is deregulated. New England Power, for example, sold its Canadian supplies into the third party gas market and used coal and oil in its generating plants last winter. By doing so, the utility maintained 100% load factor on its gas contracts through the winter months and mitigated its transportation charges by 35% to 40%. The same panel suggested that with the end of the electric utility monopoly, the market is likely to see more competitive electric prices, causing some users to switch from natural gas. Both demand

and price for natural gas will drop in the interim as the barriers go down in the power market and more efficient use translates to lower electric prices.

A February 1994 report by National Economic Research Associates, Inc. (White Plaines, NY) concluded the price of natural gas overtook and passed that of residential fuel oil in 1993, but the positions should reverse themselves again in the next few years. The prices of natural gas and heavy oil remained below the high costs of the 1980s. NERA forecasted steady increases in natural gas consumption and prices over the next 10 years, but probably not as sharply as those of oil. NERA reported that the U.S. gas market totalled about 20.2 trillion cubic feet in 1993. Meanwhile, the wellhead gas price rose slightly more than 14%. The organization predicted an average U.S. wellhead gas price of $2.09 million cubic feet this year. One factor in this growth is expected to be rapid growth in gas use in the electric utilities throughout the 1995 to 2010 period. NERA also foresaw net imports of natural gas, primarily from Canada, to increase from 1993's 2.1 trillion cubic feet to 3.25 trillion cubic feet in 2005 and to 3.6 trillion cubic feet in 2010.

According to Bonneville Power Administration's A. Smith, in addressing the 1994 Cogen Turbo Power Congress and Exposition (Atlanta), coal-based combustion plants are no longer considered in the mix of the Pacific Northwest's energy resources. The emphasis is on cogeneration systems which produce very low emissions. At the same meeting, A.T. Donnelly of Barakat & Chamberlain (Portland, OR) said that natural gas prices will remain stable in the Pacific Northwest in the near future. Natural gas is the new standard in the Pacific Northwest's power competition.

13.3 Short Term Outlook

According to the EIA, utility gas demand is expected to increase an additional 3.5% in 1995, from 8.0% in 1994. Demand for gas by nonutility generators is expected to increase 6.2% in 1995. EIA projects that monthly natural gas capacity will be able to meet projected demand throughout 1995. The increase in drilling in 1994 is expected to reverse a declining trend in wellhead productive capacity that began in the mid-1980s. The increased drilling was a result of projected higher gas prices.

According to JTB & Associates (San Diego, CA), a total of 2,125 MW of new coal-fired generation capacity is scheduled to be commissioned in the United States in 1995.

Additional Clean Coal Technology projects will go online in 1995. Thirteen projects are scheduled to go online in 1994 and 1995.

13.4 Mid-Range and Long Term Outlook

In the *Annual Energy Outlook 1994*, the 'Reference Case' assumes an annual economic growth rate of 2%; electric power generation by fuel type for electric utilities is forecast by the Energy Information Administration of the DoE as follows (1992 data provided for reference):

- 1992
  Coal: 1,576 billion kWh
  Petroleum: 89 billion kWh
  Natural gas: 264 billion kWh
  Nuclear power: 619 billion kWh
  Pumped storage and other: -4 billion kWh
  Renewable sources: 254 billion kWh
  Total: 2,798 billion kWh

- 2000
  Coal: 1,687 billion kWh
  Petroleum: 85 billion kWh
  Natural gas: 335 billion kWh
  Nuclear power: 671 billion kWh
  Pumped storage and other: -11 billion kWh
  Renewable sources: 305 billion kWh
  Total: 3,072 billion kWh

- 2010 (annual growth 1992-2101 in parenthesis)
  Coal: 1,886 billion kWh (1.0%)
  Petroleum: 74 billion kWh (-1.0%)
  Natural gas: 373 billion kWh (1.9%)
  Nuclear power: 612 billion kWh (-0.1%)
  Pumped storage and other: -11 billion kWh (5.8%)
  Renewable sources: 326 billion kWh (1.4%)
  Total: 3,260 billion kWh (0.9%)

For the Reference Case, generation by fuel type for non-utility generators is

forecast as follows (1992 data provided for reference):

- 1992
  Coal: 2 billion kWh
  Petroleum/other: 1 billion kWh
  Natural gas: 16 billion kWh
  Renewable sources: 40 billion kWh
  Total: 60 billion kWh

- 2000
  Coal: 9 billion kWh
  Petroleum/other: 1 billion kWh
  Natural gas: 72 billion kWh
  Renewable sources: 69 billion kWh
  Total: 151 billion kWh

- 2010 (annual growth 1992-2101 in parenthesis)
  Coal: 54 billion kWh (22.0%)
  Petroleum/other: 0 billion kWh (-4.9%)
  Natural gas: 144 billion kWh (13.0%)
  Renewable sources: 139 billion kWh (7.1%)
  Total: 338 billion kWh (10.1%)

Coal-fired plants continue to account for more than half of total electricity generation. However, the share of generation contributed by gas-fired plants, both utility and non-utility, increases significantly. By 2010, gas-fired plants will surpass nuclear as the second most important generating resource. While utilities still continue to depend on coal-fired plants and increase their reliance of gas-fired plants, they are also expected to make investments in demand-side management programs.

The Energy Information Administration forecasts a rise in the fuel cost component of electricity ranging between 1.3% and 2.0%, depending upon five scenarios:

- Reference case: 1.8%
- High economic growth case: 2.0%
- Low economic growth case: 1.5%
- High oil price case: 1.9%
- Low oil price case: 1.3%

The rise in fuel costs is attributed mainly to an increased reliance on natural gas to produce electricity. The reference, high economic growth, and low economic growth cases assume annual economic growth rates of 2%, 2.4%, and 1.6%, respectively, and a mid-path for the world oil price. The oil price scenarios assume an annual economic growth rate of 2% and assume oil prices may increase from $19 per barrel in 1991 to $38 per barrel in 2010 (high oil price case) or fall to $14 per barrel in 1999 and then rise to about $18 per barrel by 2010 (low oil price case).

By 2005, the consumption of natural gas for electric power generation is expected to double from 1990 levels. By 2010, the price of natural gas is expected to have nearly doubled relative to its 1990 price. (During the same period, the price of coal is only expected to increase by 30%). Thus, the price increase of natural gas will have a large impact on the fuel component of the price of electricity. If the economy grows more rapidly, as assumed in the High Economic Growth Case, higher fuel and purchased power costs will cause electricity prices to increase. Although higher economic growth will result in significant increases in the need for new capacity for utilities, the impact on capital costs per kWh is insignificant because the effect of the increased asset base (ratebase) is offset by a lower rate of return on invested assets and higher electricity sales. The lower rate of return is the result of lower borrowing costs and lower returns on the equity component of the cost of capital.

According to JTB & Associates (San Diego, CA), scheduled U.S. capacity additions for coal and waste coal are:

- 1996: 2,595 MW
- 1997: 1,231 MW
- 1998:   440 MW
- 1999: 1,785 MW
- 2000: 1,268 MW

According to the Energy Information Administration, the electricity sector will account for 97% of the increase in total U.S. coal consumption by 2010. Of the increased distribution of coal to this sector, 166 million short tons (or 81%) are projected to be met by coal producers west of the Mississippi. Net additions to coal-fired power plant capacity will occur primarily after 2005, although utilities and non-utilities together should increase net coal capacity by about 10 GW by 2005. Through 2005, increases in coal consumption for electricity generation occur mainly as a result of increased utilization of coal-fired power plants. Nevertheless, with coal-fired power plants representing the largest share of total U.S. generating capability, coal is expected to continue fueling 47% of the nation's total electricity requirements in 2005.

The Clean Coal Technology program is developing demonstration projects that should help meet the demands for energy growth and environmental protection in the 21st century. The program was in 1986, and will see over $6 billion invested in about 50 projects when completed. About 60% of funding is from industrial participants.

The U.S. Department of Energy, Energy Information Agency (EIA), forecasts that coal will continue to dominate as the main source for U.S. power generation at least through 2010. EIA expects coal consumption for generating electricity to reach 1.1 billion tons per annum in that year. To realize the overall growth in consumption estimated by EIA, coal technologies must respond to energy and environmental demands. Developments of the Clean Coal Technology program will help. Four advanced generation products hold promise for future commercial use:

- Integrated-gasification combined-cycle
- Pressurized fluidized-bed combustion
- Externally fired combined-cycle
- Integrated-gasification fuel cell

EIA predicts 172 GW of new capacity will be needed by 2010, to meet increased demand for electricity and to offset generating unit retirements. The agency estimates new coal-steam units will account for 25% of this new capacity. The 172 GW does not include additions from plant life extensions, repowering, increased imports or supplies from cogenerators. EIA also predicts existing baseload capacity will be fully utilized after 2000, and utilities will recommence constructing more coal-fired, baseload plants. EIA believes 77% of the new coal-fired plants will be brought on-line after 2000. Although

EIA projects coal plant capacity growth at only about 1.1% annually through 2010, it projects coal will continue to dominate electric generation, with its share falling only slightly to 54% by the end of the period. EIA also predicts non-utility generators will increase their share of power generated from coal from 2.6% in 1993 to 16% in 2010.

For the period 1993 to 2000, EIA predicts utilities will switch from high-sulfur coals to medium- and low-sulfur types to comply with CAAA, as some already have. The agency predicts utility demand for low-sulfur coal, mainly from the west, will rise by 148 million short tons between 1990 and 2000.

With the fuel of choice being coal in many situations, the effort accelerates to gasify it to burn cleaner and more efficiently. According to The McIlvaine Company (Northbrook, IL), there are at least 55 coal gas-fired power projects planned or under construction worldwide. Of those, 15 are in the United States. The market over the next decade exceeds $100 billion.

According to Industrial Information Services (Reno, NV), excellent growth in coal consumption by U.S. electric utilities is expected, from 793 million tons in 1993 to 891 million tons in 2000. Between 1993 and 2000, utilities consumption of low-sulfur coal will be up by 104 million tons and medium-sulfur coal consumption will rise 58 million tons.

The Energy Information Administration projects the use of coal for power generation will increase through the year 2010, accounting for slightly less than 54% of generation in that year. However, natural gas will continue its trend of gaining an increasing share of the electric generation market.

According to the American Gas Association, natural gas consumption in the United States will grow twice as rapidly as overall primary energy consumption, and will increase its market share. By 2010, the United States will consume 25.4 quadrillion Btus (quads) of natural gas annually, representing an average annual growth rate of 1.4% per year. Overall, U.S. primary energy use will grow only 0.65% per year through 2010, and will reach a level of 95.3 quads in 2010. Natural gas consumption for electricity generation will grow substantially. Consumption by electric utilities will climb to 4.8 quads by 2010, up 67.4% from current levels. Use by cogenerators and independent power plants will grow to 3.9 quads by 2010, over three times more than what is being used at present. While the total amount of natural gas used for generating electricity in 2010 will be quite large, 8.7 quads, it will represent only 19.2% of all energy used for electricity generation, and will not equal the 1970 market share of 26.9%.

According to the Energy Information Administration, increased gas consumption is driven largely by new markets for natural gas, with most of the increase attributed to electricity generation by cogenerators, electric utilities, IPPs, and EWGs. Residential and commercial sector consumption remain relatively stable, with industrial sector consumption growing by more than 25% and utility sector consumption nearly doubling. Utility-sector growth is driven by both greater use of existing plants and a substantial increase in combined-cycle plants over the forecast period, with combined-cycle capacity increasing from 5.7 GW in 1990 to 35.4 GW in 2010. The significant utility-sector increase is due in part to the impact of the Clean Air Act Amendments of 1990, tightened state environmental regulations stemming from local environment and health concerns, and the increased confidence that natural gas is now plentiful and will remain competitive with oil product alternatives in the mid- to long term.

According to the *1994 Energy Service Report*, published by ICF Kaiser International, Inc. (Fairfax, VA), recent natural gas and coal price increases are short-term peaks and will not last. Other fuel competition will limit long-term oil prices to a narrower range than expected. Long-term market fundamentals support a moderate growth outlook for natural gas and a declining to flat growth outlook for coal prices. Since there are plenty of low-cost gas resources available, as use can be expected to increase substantially in the electric power generation market. Competition between eastern and western low-sulfur coals, SO_2 scrubbers and SO_2 allowance purchases along with continuing productivity improvements will prevent further increases in the coal market. Due to the fact that oil prices are uncertain, there is a price floor at about $10 to $12 per barrel and a price ceiling at $23 to $27 per barrel.

Known world oil reserves are currently at about 30 years. However, according to Global Business Network (Washington, DC), it is very unlikely that we will begin to run out of oil before another 50 or 60 years.

According to Energy Ventures Analysis (Arlington, VA), natural gas will not be the fuel of choice for utilities during the 21st century. Recent trends favoring natural gas use for steam electric peaking power and for cogeneration will erode under the pressures of rising natural gas prices, increased capacity factors at coal baseload units and intensified competition in the electric utility industry, according to the EVA study.

13.5 Opportunities

An emerging technology with good potential for future utility installation is fluidized bed combustion (FBC). According to SFA Pacific, Inc. (Mountain View, CA), FBC technology has now become a major competitor for conventional solid fuel combustion systems worldwide. In the United States, independent power producers and cogenerators have led the way in deploying FBC boilers for electric power generation. Utility type reheat units of 115 MW to 165 MW are now in operation in the United States and Europe. The market leaders are Ahlstrom Pyropower (144 units sold, 48,344 Mlb/hr capacity), Tampella Power (41 units, 12,602 Mlb/hr), Lurgi (27 units, 12,038 Mlb/hr), ABB Combustion Engineering (23 units, 12,009 Mlb/hr), Foster Wheeler Energy Corporation (41 units, 9,382 Mlb/hr), and Deutsche Babcock (35 units, 8,411 Mlb/hr). The market for fluidized-bed technology looks promising. According to SFA, an increasing number of electric utilities are evaluating the technology, and by 2010, they expect to see a couple of 200 MW to 300 MW circulating FBC reheat units in operation in the United States.

14 NUCLEAR POWER

CONTENTS:

14.1 Trends and Market Assessment
14.2 Recent Activities
14.3 Short Term Outlook
14.4 Mid-Range and Long Term Outlook
14.5 Opportunities

14.1 Trends and Market Assessment

At the beginning of 1994, there were 109 nuclear generating plants in operation in the United States.

Utilities have not placed any new orders for nuclear power plants since 1978 and have cancelled 62 that were previously placed. The last year a nuclear plant was ordered and not subsequently cancelled was 1974.

Asian countries plan more aggressive nuclear energy development than any other area of the globe, according to the Nuclear Energy Institute. Japan, South Korea, China, and Taiwan are in the forefront of these plans with 14 units already under construction.

Worldwide, the slowing of growth in nuclear power is expected to continue. Concerns about safety, waste disposal, and construction costs will cloud future development. The Energy Information Administration projects worldwide nuclear capacity to grow to a total capacity of somewhere between 339 gigawatts and 413 gigawatts by 2010. At the beginning of 1994, there were 420 operable units in 30 countries, with a total capacity of 329 gigawatts. The three countries with the most projected capacity additions are Japan, South Korea and France. Several countries, particularly in Western Europe, are expected to have less capacity than they have now.

Worldwide, 14% of existing reactors have passed the midpoint in their design lives (assuming a 40-year life). In the United States, the commercial reactors that have been retired have average operating lifetimes of less than 20 years each.

14.2 Recent Activities

In March 1994, the Energy Information Administration released its statistics on 1993 power generation by utilities. Nuclear power contributed 21.2% of net utility generation in the United States, or about 600,000 gigawatts. This was approximately 1% less than in 1992, and the first time since 1980 that nuclear generation decreased from the previous year. Several nuclear units had major refueling maintenance or repair outages.

According to the Edison Electric Institute, nuclear plant capital expenditures by U.S. investor-owned utilities were $2.67 billion in 1994.

In December 1994, the Tennessee Valley Authority announced that it would not complete construction of three partially built nuclear units because of prohibitively high costs, TVA's huge debt, and competitive changes in the power industry. The units are the 1,170 MW Watts Bar Unit 2, and twin 1,330 MW Bellefonte Units 1 and 2. Costs have already reached $6.3 billion and another $8.8 billion would be needed to complete construction. TVA once had the nation's biggest nuclear reactor construction program. But the program had become too big and too expensive. Total investment was nearly $25 billion. Since 1982, TVA had scrapped nine reactors and literally rebuilt others in an attempt to solve vexing problems with design, materials, and workmanship. In a reversal of policy, TVA decided nuclear power would no longer be its cornerstone for growth. "Its time to take a decisive, responsible action to leave these outdated policies behind," TVA Chairman Craven Crowell said.

A new generation of nuclear plants began to enter the marketplace in 1994. The Nuclear Regulatory Commission gave their final design approvals to the General Electric ABWR system on 13 July 1994 and to the ABB-CE System 80+ on 26 July 1994. The design approvals mean that all major design and safety issues are resolved, and both companies can proceed into the certification phase of the licensing process.

Doubt was cast on the feasibility of Yucca Mountain (Nevada) as a permanent high-level waste storage facility in 1994 when the U.S. Geological Survey found a new fault. Designated as the 'Sundance Fault,' the location is near the already known Ghost Dance fault.

A technical paper presented by J. Redding and C. Veitch of General Electric at the 1994 winter meeting of the Nuclear Power Society (Washington, DC) concluded that nuclear electricity is the least cost option when you include environmental externalities. At present, the least cost option is generally considered a natural gas combined-cycle plant that generates electricity at between 3.5 cents/kWh and 4.0 cents/kWh. Right now, however, nuclear power's average cost is about 7 cents/kwh. Of the total cost of electricity produced by an advanced nuclear plant, the capital costs are about 67%; operating and maintenance costs are about 17%, and fuel costs are about 12% (decommissioning and spent fuel storage account for the rest). Approximately two-thirds of the capital cost, and roughly 80% of the total costs, according to Redding and Veitch, are fixed. That means the variable costs of a new nuclear power plant are around 20%. A combined-cycle plant's costs are essentially the opposite. The kicker that would dramatically change the evaluation of competing technologies in a least cost analysis, according to Redding and Veitch, are environmental externalities. Studies by GE show that when externalities are used in evaluating options for the future (operation in 2002), the cost of fossil-fueled electricity increases to the point where nuclear power becomes the least-cost option with a 1 cent/kWh advantage.

The construction of new nuclear plants proceeded in Asia in 1994. According to *Electric Light & Power*, In Japan, construction of Kashiwazaki-Kariwa Units 6 and 7 is proceeding on schedule. These 1,350 MW General Electric Nuclear Energy units are almost identical to the company's Advanced Boiling Water Reactor (ABWR) proposed for the U.S. utilities. The Japanese Units 6 and 7 should be ready for commercial operation by Tokyo Electric Power Company in 1996 and 1997, respectively.

Taiwan Power Company is in the midst of negotiating for new generation nuclear generating plants with ABB Combustion Engineering (ABB-CE), Westinghouse Electric and Framatone of France. There are rumors that negotiations are underway for a contract to be signed soon for an ABB-CE System 80+ reactor plant to be constructed in

South Korea.

The Mescalero Apache Tribe (New Mexico) announced plans for the first private temporary storage facility for spent nuclear fuel rods. A meeting of officials of 30 utilities was held at the reservation on 10 March 1994 to develop support for the project, which would be industry funded. The facility would provide temporary storage for up to 10,000 tons of spent nuclear fuel and would cost $100 million. Northern States Power Company signed a tentative agreement with the tribe on 03 February 1994 to store spent nuclear rods at the facility.

Dismantling of the Fort St. Vrain generating unit (Colorado) began in 1994. The Public Utilities Commission of the State of Colorado issued authorization in June 1994 for the plant to be repowered as a gas-fired combined cycle steam plant consisting of two turbines and two heat recovery steam generators.

The U.S. Department of Energy's Office of Fusion Energy spent $347.6 million on nuclear fusion research in FY1994.

14.3 Short Term Outlook

In view of the desperate need for means to dispose of spent nuclear fuel, the most closely watched development will be a lawsuit by 14 nuclear utilities headed by Northern State's Power, 20 state governments, and several state public utility commissions which would force the U.S. Department of Energy to "clarify its obligation" to make available a temporary monitored retrievable storage facility for nuclear waste by 1998. DoE has already collected $10 billion from nuclear utilities' ratepayers to finance this project and plans to open a permanent storage site by 2010. According to industry sources, the suits seek the following action: a court ruling that the Nuclear Waste Policy Act require the DoE to begin taking title to and removing spent nuclear fuel from nuclear power plants in 1998, court-mandated monitoring of the DoE's nuclear waste management program so it will be ready to accept fuel by 1998, and to allow ratepayer payments to the Nuclear Waste Fund be put in escrow in an effort to better control those funds.

The Edison Electric Institute expects utility expenditures for nuclear plant construction in the United States to decrease 20.6% to $2.19 billion in 1995. These expenditures, of course, are at existing plants, and not new construction.

According to CRS Market Data Services (Tulsa, OK), electric utilities in the United States and Canada are planning 67 refueling outages at nuclear power plants between October 1994 and April 1997, with an expenditure of nearly $2 billion for nuclear fuel. An additional $295 million will be spent on maintenance. The nuclear fuel expenditure will be about $800 million in 1995.

Though construction still requires congressional approval, the Clinton administration has authorized preliminary design of a $1.8 billion installation to simulate nuclear weapon tests while advancing development of fusion as an inexhaustible power source. The Department of Energy plans to solicit queries in early 1995 from consultants for the National Ignition Facility. The current timetable calls for construction during 1996 and 2002.

While no new nuclear construction will occur in the United States in 1995, nuclear construction will continue its growth in Asia. In all, about 100 nuclear plants worldwide are still in the construction pipeline -- that is, either under construction or planned.

14.4 Mid-Range and Long Term Outlook

There will be little or no change in nuclear generation in the United States for the next few years. Then, depending on the resolution of issues related to the repair and relicensing of some of the oldest reactors, U.S. nuclear generating capacity will begin to decline relatively in the late 1990s and absolutely in the early years of the 21st century.

It has been estimated that more than half of the nuclear reactors which operate in the United States will have run out of storage space for spent fuel by 2010.

Although there have been no new orders for nuclear power plants that have not been subsequently cancelled in almost 20 years, manufacturers would like to resume plant construction. To that end, the industry is developing new standard plant designs that include advanced light-water reactors (ALWRs), which are classified as either evolutionary or mid-sized advanced plants, and non-LWR modular advanced designs. The evolutionary designs, producing about 1,300 MW per unit, are improved versions of the LWR plants currently in operation. They incorporate engineering safety features that are simpler, relative to those in current LWRs, as well as technological advances. The overall design of these evolutionary plants includes passive safety features that provide operators with increased time (over existing plants) to respond appropriately to safety-related events. The mid-size ALWR designs also build on current LWR technology; at

600 MW, however, they are roughly one-half the size of the evolutionary plant designs.

Competition will become the slogan for the U.S. nuclear industry. Electricity production will become fiercely competitive and only the most efficient, lowest-cost producers will survive and grow. Other American industries have already learned this lesson, tightened their belts, and honed their efficiency. Now it is the nuclear energy industry's turn, according to Phillip Bayne, president of the U.S. Council for Energy Awareness, an international trade organization of nuclear energy industries. The council has developed an industry-wide Strategic Plan to Improve Economic Performance. This plan is a catalyst for increasing effectiveness within nuclear plants, to cut operating and maintenance costs.

Nuclear generating plant construction expenditures will continue to drop sharply in the near future. The Edison Electric Institute forecasts an expenditure of $1.88 billion in 1996, a drop of about 30% from the 1994 level.

Finding a means of disposal for radioactive waste will continue to be the hottest issue in the industry. The federal government has committed to accept radioactive waste on an interim storage basis by 1998, however, it is not certain that this obligation will be met. If DoE delays its commitment to take spent nuclear fuel again, some nuclear plants will face shutdown or construction of additional on-site storage. The U.S. Department of Energy has advanced studies of its planned underground repository at Yucca Mountain (Nevada), but it is unlikely that it can receive fuel before 2010. Despite controversies, Yucca Mountain remains the most promising site for a permant repository

An equally critical problem also exists in disposal of low-level radioactive wastes.

There are only two active sites in the United States, Hanford, WA and Barnwell County, SC, and both accept waste only from regional facilities. Three other facilities are planned but no construction has begun.

Twenty-four of the nation's 107 operating commercial nuclear units are expected to shut down within the next decade, and virtually all of them by 2020, according to the Electric Power Research Institute (Palo Alto, CA). Worldwide, 500 reactors will be candidates for decommissioning during the same period.

Nuclear fusion still presents a good possibility for serving as a future energy source. One of the main advantages of the fusion reaction is that the small amount of resulting radioactive waste is short-lived. Another is that if anything goes wrong, the reaction stops working by itself. The United States has spent $10 billion on fusion research so far, but progress has been slow because of the difficulties of handling and maintaining the plasma and reaction within it.

14.5 Opportunities

There will be multi-billion dollar opportunities in and for dismantling nuclear facilities which have shut down and relicensing nuclear plants which are to remain in operation.

One estimate has put the cost of dismantling all U.S. nuclear steam supply systems at over $20 billion. Commonwealth Edison, the largest nuclear operator in the U.S., estimated the cost of decommissioning its 13 plants, with a total capacity of 12,000 MW, at $2.8 billion. This estimate has been called unrealistically low by some estimates. Dismantling requires some means of disposal of the radioactive waste. An alternative is mothballing plants. With safe storage, a reactor can decontaminate for 50 years or more, considerably reducing the cost of subsequent dismantling and disposal. The initial cost of safe storage has been estimated at $20 million to $40 million per MW, plus $3 million to $10 million per MW annually thereafter for maintenance.

The cost to relicense a nuclear plant has been estimated at more than $1 billion. In the U.S., a utility must decide about 10 years before a nuclear unit's 40 year operating license expires whether it will seek relicensing or shut down. So far, no U.S. reactor has remained in use for its licensed lifetime, and no utility has decided to seek relicensing.

15 HYDROELECTRIC

CONTENTS:

15.1 Trends and Market Assessment
15.2 Recent Activities
15.3 Short Term Outlook
15.4 Mid-Range and Long Term Outlook
15.5 Opportunities

15.1 Trends and Market Assessment

The Federal Energy Regulatory Administration publishes *Hydroelectric Power Resources of the United States* every four years. The most recent publication was in 1992, and presents data on the capacity, generation, and other characteristics of the developed and undeveloped hydroelectric power resources of the United States. It is the only single source of such data. The following is a summary of the FERC data. Pumped storage plants are included as well as conventional hydroelectric plants.

The total developed hydroelectric capacity in the U.S. as of 01 January 1992 was 91,600 MW. There were 2,304 conventional plants in operation, including those with combined pumped storage, providing approximately 73,500 MW of developed capacity. There was an additional 18.1 MW of pumped storage capacity. There were 1,809 constructed hydroelectric plants under FERC license, and 55,300 MW in FERC-authorized capacity. Capacity at federal projects was 46,850 MW. The balance of capacity is exempted from licensing.

According to the Energy Information Administration, hydroelectric generation (excluding pumped storage) was 247.88 billion kilowatt hours in 1992.

Hydropower is no less environmentally compatible than any other renewable for a given amount of generation; however, hydropower owners must face enormous environmental scrutiny and mitigation before their projects can be developed. The licensing process brings non-federal dams that are used for hydropower under the jurisdiction of the FERC, subjecting them to intense scrutiny when they would otherwise be uncontrolled. In order to obtain a license, hydropower applicants spend an average of $1 million for environmental studies, and as much as another $1 million in mitigation measures to license a 10 MW hydropower project. This effectively doubles the cost of creating hydroelectricity for the first ten years of the license.

The smallest hydro projects, developed between 1978 and 1986, ranged from 10 kW to 20 MW of output capacity. Changes in utility private power purchase processes, the increased complexity and expense of hydro power plant permitting, and environmental impact assessment and licensing since 1987 have pushed developers to increase the size of small hydro projects to justify higher project development costs, protect project profitability and minimize unit energy costs. As a result, the vast majority of small hydro projects under development between 1987 to 1992 ranged from 2 MW to 50 MW in output capacity.

15.2 Recent Activities

In March 1994, the Energy Information Administration released its statistics on 1993 power generation by utilities. Hydroelectric generation accounted for 9.2% of net utility generation in the United States, or about 265,000 gigawatts. This was an increase of about 11% over 1992. Record rainfall in some parts of the United States contributed to this large gain.

Much of the recent rehabilitation and modernization work of hydroelectric facilities has been motivated by the active programs for site relicensing by hydropower site licenses throughout the United States. Projects in 1994 were in anticipation of licenses which are scheduled to expire in the next few years:

- 1995: four projects, 75 MW
- 1996: seven projects, 40 MW
- 1997: five projects, 290 MW
- 1998: six projects, 160 MW

One of the initiatives of President Clinton's Global Change Action Plan, put in place in 1994, is for private investment to upgrade output of existing hydroelectric facilities in exchange for lease payments to sell the extra generation. This will raise $2.7 billion between 1994 to 2000.

15.3 Short Term Outlook

Considerable new construction for hydroelectric generating facilities in the United States will continue in 1995. According to FERC, construction was underway on 1,900

MW of FERC-authorized capacity and 350 MW of federal capacity as of 01 January 1992.

According to the U.S. Department of Commerce, more than 440 MW of new capacity is expected to come on-line in the 1995 to 1997 period.

An $840 million pumped storage power project is scheduled for May 1995 completion in north Georgia by Oglethorpe Power. It will be the first pumped storage project in the U.S. since Duke Power's 1,068 MW Bad Creek installation in 1990. None are currently under construction in the U.S., but private developers plan at least six, ranging up to 2,000 MW in capacity.

A 1,000 MW pumped storage project is planned for Hunters Field, NY. Alpyn Creek Development Corporation plans to start construction in 1995. This facility will be different from conventional pumped storage projects; once the reservoir is filled, it will recycle the same water.

Mead Energy (Las Vegas, NV) is constructing a $1.25 billion, 1,000 MW hydroelectric plant on Hoover Dam's Lake Mead reservoir. Construction will be complete in 1997 or 1998. The lake will be the plant's lower reservoir. A new 400-ft. high dam, 600 ft. above the lake, will form the 65,000 acre-ft. upper reservoir in a natural geological depression. An underground power plant will house four 250 MW reversible pump turbines and generators. FERC has issued a preliminary permit to proceed with development.

A $1.8 billion, 2,000 MW pumped storage project is being built by Mt. Hope

Hydro, Inc. (Dover, NJ) at the site of an abandoned, flooded iron mine in Rockaway Township, NJ. The licensing process took seven years and required 54 separate submissions to FERC. Construction started at the end of 1993 and should be completed by 1998. Stone & Webster Engineering Corporation is the project manager and designer, which involves digging deep shafts and excavating a large reservoir 2,800 ft. below the ground. The plant will be the largest-capacity private power and the second-largest pumped storage plant in the United States.

15.4 Mid-Range and Long Term Outlook

In the *Annual Energy Outlook 1994*, for the 'Reference Case,' which assumes an annual economic growth rate of 2%, conventional hydroelectric capacity and electric power generation in the United States are forecast as follows:

- 2000
  Capacity: 78.29 gigawatts
  Generation: 305.07 billion kilowatt hours

- 2005
  Capacity: 78.43 gigawatts
  Generation: 305.89 billion kilowatt hours

- 2010 (annual growth 1992-2101 in parenthesis)
  Capacity: 78.53 gigawatts (0.2%)
  Generation: 306.58 billion kilowatt hours (1.3%)

With the decline in new hydro construction in the United States, repowering and refurbishing will be the most rapidly growing part of the hydro business throughout the remainder of the 1990s. Black & Veatch, for example, reports 40% of their hydro business is in this area. A study conducted by the Bonneville Power Administration concluded that, considering total lifetime costs, efficiency improvements in existing hydroelectric facilities was the single most cost-effective means of increasing capacity.

Most hydroelectric plants in the United States started operating in the first half of the 20th century. Today's turbines can provide up to 15% more energy than their ancestors of the 1920s and 1930s, with the same available water. Other powerhouse components have improved efficiency as well, especially exciters, generators and transformers. Automated controls and operating techniques are now available to optimize the use of water flow so the maximum power is generated at the most beneficial times.

The hydropower refurbishment market is, in fact, two related sub-markets. With its primary focus on evaluating, upgrading, or rehabilitating dams, the first submarket involves extensive civil engineering work, principally the result of regulatory compliance orders by the FERC. This work involves probable maximum flood (PMF) studies, Part 12 dam safety inspections, physical expansion of spillway capacity, and the design and management of improvements to dam stability, including post-tensioned anchoring.

The second sub-market, which involves equipment upgrading and modernization, is divided into several elements: turbine upgrade, runner or water distribution parts replacement, generator rewinds, and automation or control system upgrades.

15.5 Opportunities

There is much opportunity for expanded hydropower development in the United

States. Total undeveloped potential hydroelectric capacity in the United States as of 01 January 1992 was 73,200 MW. This does not include potential pumped storage capacity. Retired hydropower plant sites also offer a significant potential for redevelopment. According to FERC, there are 2,887 retired plants in the United States; 2,025 sites offer a redevelopment potential totaling 1,237 megawatts.

Opportunities for new hydroelectric power development in developing nations will exceed activity in the United States. Where appropriate natural conditions exist to make it feasible, governments of many developing countries consider hydroelectricity an important vehicle in guaranteeing a secure source of electricity and, thereby ensure continued economic development and an accompanying rise in living standards. The development of hydroelectricity is, nevertheless, constrained by the high costs associated with installation (which include building dams and rerouting water passages) and by recent concerns over effects of hydroelectric facilities on the environment. A number of hydroelectric power projects are currently underway throughout the developing world. The Chinese government has announced plans to build five hydroelectric dams by the year 2000, including the Three Gorges Project; a $20 billion, 18,000 megawatt project. A major objective in China is to provide rural electrification to regions that are now deficient in energy. In Central and South America, hydroelectricity is the second largest contributor to the energy supply of the region (exceeding natural gas, coal, and nuclear power); it was responsible for 27% of all primary energy there in 1992. The development potential for hydroelectricity is greatest in Brazil, Colombia, Venezuela, and Argentina; and these countries have strategic policies to increase the already significant share of total electricity output it provides. Brazil is currently expanding two major hydroelectric plants, including the Itaipu station (a joint effort with Paraguay), which is already the largest hydroelectric dam project in the world. These two plants will have a combined capacity of 20,000 megawatts. Brazil currently gets 96% of its electricity from its rivers, and is continuing hydroelectric development despite growing opposition from environmental groups.

16 BIOMASS AND WASTE-TO-ENERGY

CONTENTS:

16.1 Trends and Market Assessment
16.2 Recent Activities
16.3 Short Term Outlook
16.4 Mid-Range and Long Term Outlook
16.5 Opportunities

16.1 Trends and Market Assessment

Biomass is defined as any organic matter available on a renewable basis for conversion to energy, including forest residues, agricultural crops and waste, wood and wood wastes, animal wastes, aquatic plants, and municipal wastes.

In the United States, bioenergy accounts for roughly 4% of total energy use. The primary uses of bioenergy in the United States are industrial cogeneration, primarily in the pulp and paper industry, and residential heating by wood stoves. Municipal solid waste and ethanol provide most of the remaining bioenergy.

Among renewable energy resources, biomass is one of the most promising, with the potential to provide electricity through combustion, gasification, and biochemical processes, as well as supplying gaseous and liquid fuels that can compete with conventional energy sources in large-scale applications. The production of biomass for energypurposes can also offer environmental benefits. The most notable is the potential for providing energy with little or no net buildup of carbon dioxide in the atmosphere if the biomass is produced renewably. Biomass also has the potential to help revitalize the rural sector of the economy.

The U.S. DoE, in its May 1992 analysis of energy from municipal solid waste (MSW), concluded that as an energy resource, MSW is unique. It can be used to produce energy, displace fossil fuels and improve the environment by reducing the amount of wastes that must be landfilled, and by conserving energy and natural resources. In addition, because MSW is considered a renewable biomass fuel, it meets most state public utility commission requirements for alternative fuel usage. Moreover, as a domestic resource, energy dollars and their positive effect on the economy are kept at home.

Revenues to waste-to-energy (WTE) plants in the U.S. from the sale of electricity are approximately $800 million per year, and total annual revenues are approximately $2 billion. This does not include industrial facilities, which burn on-site wastes to generate electrical power. Energy sales generally account for 35% to 50% of a WTE facility's revenues. Other revenues include the facility's tipping fee and sale of materials recycled on-site. According to the Integrated Waste Services Association (Washington, DC), there are 142 existing WTE facilities operating in the United States, with a net capacity of 86,100 tons per day. They burn 31 million tons of trash (about 15% of U.S. trash) and produce 17.3 million MWh of electricity per year. Electricity generated from solid waste typically has a value of $.02 to $.08. per kWh. About 70 of the 142 facilities have recycling as part of their operations.

According to the Integrated Waste Services Association (Washington, DC), there are 142 existing WTE facilities operating in the United States, with a net capacity of 86,100 tons per day. They burn 31 million tons of trash (about 15% of U.S. trash) and produce 17.3 million MWh of electricity per year. Electricity generated from solid waste typically has a value of $.02 to $.08. per kWh.

According to *Environmental Business Journal* (San Diego, CA), the waste-to-energy business has been up and down in the 1990s. More than 100 projects have been cancelled, but new projects under construction and in planning are expected to provide the added capacity to handle nearly 25% of municipal solid waste by 2000.

16.2 Recent Activities

On 02 May 1994, the U.S. Supreme Court ruled that municipal waste combustion ash must be managed under federal hazardous waste rules. Those within the industry see minimal impact. Most plant operators and state regulators were already accustomed to some type of ash testing, and many states had already established rigid protocols for its disposal.

The paramount issue in solid waste management is flow control. On 16 May 1994, the U.S. Supreme Court struck down waste flow control as economic protectionism in violation of the Commerce Clause of the U.S. Constitution. Several local governments throughout the United States use flow control ordinances to dictate where MSW will be processed or disposed. This has implications on WTE, restricting control with municipal legislation on MSW generated locally or that which is transported into the community.

Battelle Memorial Institute (Columbus, OH) announced in 1994 the first conversion of biomass into a gas that can be used as gas turbine fuel. Wood waste was used in the initial development, but other renewables, such as crop residue, lawn clippings, residue from food manufacturing or energy crops, could be utilized.

Idaho Power Company initiated a three-year, $5 million program in 1994 to install photovoltaic systems for service to remotely situated customers.

16.3 Short Term Outlook

The waste-to-energy market is expected to continue struggling in 1995. Municipal governments will continue to subsidize trash burning efforts with taxpayer money to keep plants running at high levels.

The diminishing landfill capacity in the United States favorably influences the waste-to-energy alternative. When Subtitle D requirements are fully implemented in 1995, 3,000 municipal solid waste landfills are expected to remain open. This represents a dramatic drop. In 1980, 22,000 permitted landfills were operating in the United States; only 5,300 landfills were operating in 1990. Specifically, many sites are expected to close with the initial requirement for the posting of financial assurance in April 1995. The rate of premature closures will not be as dramatic as the hazardous waste facility closures (approximately 75% of then-existing hazardous waste facilities closed rather than post financial assurance), but there will be a significant reduction in the number of facilities due to either a reluctance or an inability to commit those funds to financial assurance. The result is that landfill costs will continue to increase. Experts predict the nation could have as few as 1,000 landfills by 2000.

Environmental Business Journal forecasts the solid waste industry will rebound slightly in 1995 and 1996, but does not expect the market to grow much beyond 5% to 6% annually. After experiencing average annual market growth rates in excess of 10% in the mid- and late-1980s, growth in the solid waste market suddenly dropped to 3% or 4% in 1991, and remained at that level through 1993.

16.4 Mid-Range and Long Term Outlook

In the *Annual Energy Outlook 1994*, the 'Reference Case' assumes an annual economic growth rate of 2%; capacity and electric power generation for municipal solid waste combustion in the United States are forecast as follows:

- 2000
  Capacity: 3.64 gigawatts
  Generation: 20.17 billion kilowatt hours

- 2005
  Capacity: 4.43 gigawatts
  Generation: 26.04 billion kilowatt hours

- 2010 (annual growth 1992-2101 in parenthesis)
  Capacity: 5.24 gigawatts (3.8%)
  Generation: 32.04 billion kilowatt hours (4.0%)

Capacity and electric power generation in the United States for biomass, excluding energy crops, are forecast as follows:

- 2000
    Capacity: 9.23 gigawatts
    Generation: 48.42 billion kilowatt hours

- 2005
    Capacity: 12.20 gigawatts
    Generation: 65.94 billion kilowatt hours

- 2010 (annual growth 1992-2101 in parenthesis)
    Capacity: 15.17 gigawatts (4.2%)
    Generation: 83.63 billion kilowatt hours (13.8%)

According to J.H. Green of Bechtel Group, Inc. (San Francisco, CA) the most likely scenario for this decade is the continued exploitation of existing sources of wood waste and agricultural residues. Fuel handling and preparation systems will continuously improve, and net plant efficiencies well over the typical 20% reported by PG&E for California biomass power plants should become the norm. Average plant capacities are expected to double in size, and improvements in steam turbine technology will have the greatest impact on plants in the 50 MW to 80 MW range. By the end of the next decade, gas turbine combined cycle or steam injected technology is expected to dominate the market.

Biomass-based power, combined with proper management of biomass production, offers major environmental benefits compared with fossil-fuel based power. Biomass power is expected to be competitive with power from conventional sources in many energy supply scenarios. Given the current political and social climate, the use of biomass for energy generation will continue and no doubt increase.

The next technology push may be gasifying biomass as turbine fuel. A group including GE Marine & Industrial Engines (Cincinnati, OH) is developing a biomass gasification turbine unit in Brazil. The team expects to start pre-commercial operation by mid-1997, consuming sugar cane waste and wood.

Ogden Projects, Inc. foresees that landfill tipping fees will rise from an average rate of $20.00 per ton in 1993 to $271.18 over the next 30 years. The use of waste-to-energy plants would reduce this to an estimated $132.76 per ton. This will serve as one of the driving forces which encourages the construction of waste-to-energy power plants.

16.5 Opportunities

Opportunities are emerging for full service WTE companies to form strategic alliances with electric utilities to develop WTE projects. For example, in 1992, Ogden Projects, Inc. formed an alliance with Ohio Edison Company to construct a WTE facility to repower two turbines on the site of the Mad River facility. The repowered project is scheduled to re-enter service in 1997. Because of waste disposal problems, the City of Atlanta asked Georgia Power Company to consider repowering a retired plant for waste-to-energy conversion. Similarly, in South Carolina, officials are looking at converting a portion of its waste stream as a fuel supplement for a local electric power plant.

Energy plantations are seriously being considered as an alternative to fossil fuels, sparked by environmental concerns about conventional forestry practices, the Clean Air Act, global climate change, soil conservation, and energy needs. While only 15,000 to 20,000 acres of short-rotation woody crops are planted in the United States today, the feedstock potential could easily lead to more than 20 GW of new capacity by 2010. Energy crops can be planted on the 200 million acres of underutilized and marginal agricultural land in the United States. Much of this land could be improved with the proper balance of biomass plantations, while at the same time generating a large renewable fuel supply. Crop set aside programs, conservation programs, emission taxes and air quality non-attainment areas have helped energy crops to become marginally competitive in some areas. Delivered energy crop production costs are now estimated at about $39 to $63/dry ton.

17 RENEWABLE ENERGY RESOURCES

CONTENTS:

17.1 Trends and Market Assessment
17.2 Recent Activities
17.3 Short Term Outlook
17.4 Mid-Range and Long Term Outlook
17.5 Opportunities

17.1 Trends and Market Assessment

The power generation sources in this chapter include the renewable sources of geothermal, solar, and wind. Fuel cells are also included, because they are an emerging energy source, although they are not renewable. Hydroelectric generation, covered in chapter 15 of this report, is not included in this chapter.

According to the Energy Information Administration, renewable energy capacity was 4.9 gigawatts in the United States in 1992, and generation was 21.34 billion kilowatt hours. The 1992 mix was distributed as follows:

- Geothermal
  Capacity: 2.89 gigawatts
  Generation: 16.68 billion kilowatt hours

- Solar (grid-connected only)
  Capacity: 0.36 gigawatts
  Generation: 1.75 billion kilowatt hours

- Wind
    Capacity: 1.65 gigawatts
    Generation: 2.91 billion kilowatt hours

The interest in alternative energy has increased in the past few years. Southern California Edison Company, for example, gets 13% of its electricity from renewable sources vs. 1% in 1985.

Utility efforts are being coordinated by the utility-funded Utility Renewable Resources Association.

Almost 14,000 wind turbines were installed in the U.S. between 1980 and 1985, totaling 1,200 MW. The vast majority were intermediate-scale (25 kW to 150 kW), privately owned, and managed by wind farm developers in California. Following the termination of tax benefits and revision of California's avoided-cost private power purchase rates, only three major wind turbine manufacturers remained and only one was producing significant amounts of turbines by 1987. About 85% of the 325 MW of capacity added to U.S. projects during the period 1986 to 1990 came from imported turbines, most in the 200 kW to 350 kW range. There was a resurgence of wind energy activity in the early 1990s and the amount of electricity generated by wind has increased substantially. In California, it increased from 2.6 billion kW in 1990 to a projected 2.9 billion kWh in 1992, an increase of almost 12%. Annual sales of wind power to California's utilities reached an estimated $220 million in 1991.

Total wind generation capacity in the United States is about 1,600 MW, far less than 1% of all U.S. power and virtually all in California. Recent generation machines are lighter, more reliable and cost less than older turbines. Installed cost of a wind farm is about $750 to $1,000 per kW; competitive with hydropower but still two to three times the cost of gas turbines.

Photovoltaics are beginning to enter the utility-connected grid. The first demonstration PV grid support system began operation on the Pacific Gas & Electric system in May 1993. A 500 kW PV system, built by Siemens Solar Industries, supports a feeder near the town of Kerman in California's Central Valley.

The current capacity of U.S. geothermal powerplants is about 2,780 MW, with a value of $3.7 billion; 2/3's of this is from steam and the balance is from hot-water reservoirs. All of it is delivered to the electric grid as base-load power.

17.2 Recent Activities

In its fiscal 1994 budget, alternative and renewable energy for the first time receive more funding than nuclear research and development. In announcing that, DoE Secretary Hazel R. O'Leary said, "We have shifted our priorities to meet the needs of a changing world."

In April 1994, the California Public Utility Commission held an auction among renewable energy producers for 14% of the state's projected electrical demand over the next 30 years, more than 1,200 MW. There is a five-year old mandate in California for renewable energy purchases.

In June 1994, Kenetech Corporation (San Francisco, CA) announced plans to erect thousands of wind turbines on sites from Oregon to Mexico at a cost of about $1 billion.

In early 1994, Sacramento Municipal Utility District (SMUD) announced plans for the first phase of a $52 million, 50 MW windfarm. Cost of power from the new wind farm is estimated to be 5 cents/kWh, competitive with conventional power plants. The new windfarm will use wind machines supplied by Kenetech Windpower. The farm is part of SMUD's plan to add 400 MW of renewable-based capacity by 2000.

In early 1994, the U.S. Army Natick Research, Development and Engineering Center (Natick, MA) announced that it would be the second military site to receive a fuel cell power plant under a federal demonstration project. A 200 kW, $18 million unit from ONSI Corporation (South Windsor, CT) will be installed.

A high-temperature solid-oxide fuel cell (SOFC) developed by Siemen's Power Generation Group established a record 1.8 kW electric power output using oxygen and hydrogen fuel, breaking the old record by 38%. Siemen's operated the SOFC for more than 300 hours without experiencing any power loss during restart.

In early 1994, the Department of Energy's Sandia National Laboratories signed a $35 million contract with Science Applications International Corporation (SAIC) to develop a 25 kW solar thermal power system for commercial utility application. According to SAIC, the non-polluting system could generate electricity for about 6 cents/kWh.

Eneron Corporation (Houston, TX) announced in late-1994 plans to build a 100-megawatt solar power plant. The plant will cost $150 million, and will be constructed on a former DoE nuclear test site in Nevada. Eneron claims it can sell power at $0.05 per kilowatt hour, and credits increased conversion efficiency and a proprietary system as key parts of its plan. Eneron also plans to build a $25 million plant to manufacture thin layers of photovoltaic modules.

Valley Electric Association, Inc. (Nye County, NV) connected a 15 kW solar cell array into its grid in 1994. The unit's manufacturer, Alpha Solarco (Cincinnati, OH), claims that if mass-produced, the solar generator could produce electricity at a cost of four to five cents per kWh, making it competitive with coal-fired power plants.

Southern California Edison Company announced in mid-1994 a pilot program that gives remote government and commercial end users the option of leasing photovoltaic arrays. Participants must install systems with at least 1 kW of capacity and expected annual electricity delivery of at least 2,000 kWh. They will lease the equipment from Edison for a period of 15 years; a buyout option can be exercised at any time.

A new solar technology, integrated high-concentration photovoltaics (IHCPV), set a world record in 1994 by achieving a solar conversion greater than 20%. Amonix, Inc. (Torrance, CA), the developer, claims the system can provide solar power at $0.06 per kilowatt hour once the cells are installed in large solar farms. The system has been assessed by the Electric Power Research Institute. According to EPRI, unlike other solar technologies using large areas of solar cells and operating at a fixed tilt toward the sun, the IHCPV system uses low-cost plastic concentrating lenses that track and focus sunlight onto small areas of solar cells. The system concentrates sunlight 200 to 500 times, which substantially reduces the amount of costly silicon cell material that would normally be required to generate a fixed amount of electricity. Earlier versions had lens which deteriorated with age, but the new system uses radiation-hardening technology developed for satellites.

M-C Power Corporation launched its 250 MW proof-of-concept molten-carbonate fuel cell (MCFC) power plant on 02 December 1994 at Unocal's Fred L. Hartley Research Center (Brea, CA). The project is open to demonstrate to industry representatives the effectiveness and efficiency of environmentally-friendly MCFC decentralized power generation plants.

There was also activity on the international front. The U.K. Department of Trade and industry announced through its Energy Minister plans to use public seed money to stimulate approximately $4.5 billion of private sector investment in renewable energy sources. The 10-year plan will focus on "good prospects" such as solar, wind and fuel cells and burning brushwood and waste materials.

17.3 Short Term Outlook

Several major alternative energy projects in the United States will be completed in 1995.

The first large demonstration of molten carbonate fuel cells will be completed and tested in mid-1995. The $46 million project by the U.S. Department of Energy is the first large-scale demonstration project of these second generation devices. The MCFC units are more efficient than phosphoric acid fuel cells, but are more costly. Phosphoric acid units cost about $3,000 per kW, compared to $23,000 per kW for this demonstration project. Fluor Daniel, Inc. (Irvine, CA) is providing engineering and construction services for the Santa Clara, CA facility.

A $1 billion solar thermal powerplant is scheduled for completion in 1995 in

Boulder City, NV. The plant will have six 80 MW units and sell generated electricity to the Nevada Power Company.

Luz International, Ltd. (Los Angeles, CA) is building a $1.4 billion solar power plant near Daggett, Southern California. The plan calls for twelve solar electric generating stations (SEGS) to be built, nine of which are complete. A joint venture has been formed with ABB Energy Ventures to complete the remaining three plants by 1995. When all of the power stations are completed, the solar capacity will be 600 MW, enough power to serve 800,000 people. The power will be sold to Southern California Edison and will produce more than 90% of the world's solar electricity.

Geothermal power projects developed during the early and mid-1990s are expected to add another 1,000 MW to cumulative power capacity installed in the United States during the period 1995 to 1999. This would represent a 31% increase in cumulative installed capacity over five years. Additional geothermal power capacity installed by U.S. firms in countries outside of the United States may reach 100 MW per year during the period 1995 to 1999, bringing total additional geothermal power capacity forecast to be built by U.S. firms to 300 MW per year over this five year period. Such a level would approach that achieved by U.S. industry during the highest growth years, 1985 to 1988.

17.4 Mid-Range and Long Term Outlook

In the *Annual Energy Outlook 1994*, the 'Reference Case' assumes an annual economic growth rate of 2%; renewable energy capacity and electric power generation in the United States are forecast as follows:

- 2000
    Capacity: 8.03 gigawatts
    Generation: 41.27 billion kilowatt hours

- 2005
    Capacity: 9.52 gigawatts
    Generation: 50.1 billion kilowatt hours

- 2010
    Capacity: 20.52 gigawatts
    Generation: 91.05 billion kilowatt hours

The capacity and generation by types of renewable sources in 2010 is forecast as follows (annual growth 1992-2101 in parenthesis):

- Geothermal
    Capacity: 8.54 gigawatts (6.2%)
    Generation: 57.15 billion kilowatt hours (7.1%)

- Solar
    Capacity: 1.33 gigawatts (7.5%)
    Generation: 4.81 billion kilowatt hours (5.8%)

- Wind
    Capacity: 10.65 gigawatts (10.9%)
    Generation: 29.09 billion kilowatt hours (13.6%)

One of the most convincing forecasts relating to the future of renewable energy is from Shell International Petroleum Company (London). Shell has had one of the best track records in forecasting the energy future, including prediction of the 1973 oil crisis. Shell's energy environment group foresees renewable energy sources growing to dominate world energy production by 2050. Two possible geopolitical scenarios were presented in the September 1994 issue of *Scientific American*. In the first scenario, the global trend toward economic liberalization and democratic reform in the 1980s continues to roll forward. This leads to a large increase in energy demand in development countries, especially China and India, the world's most populous nations. At the same time, however, energy efficiency improves because of increased competition. Energy taxes internalize environmental costs, which help to stimulate the development of cleaner technologies. In the second scenario, renewables also gain importance, but less so, in a distinctly grim setting. Regional economic and political tensions dominate the globe. Demand for oil increases, albeit slowly, but there is far less improvement in energy efficiency than in the first scheme. Protectionist policy and law weaken market forces. Oil price shocks exacerbate deteriorating international relations, and environmental anxieties spur government control of energy industries to ever stricter levels. New markets for renewables are "largely in poor countries" or are developed locally and cheaply.

The forecast of the World Energy Council (WEC) is much more conservative. The WEC considers that "new" renewable sources, which include solar, wind, small hydroelectric, modern biomass, and ocean sources, may account for only 5% of the world's energy output in 2020. In this view, fossil fuels will provide most of global energy needs through the middle of the next century, while nuclear fission plays an important supporting role. The WEC's projections, the result of a three year, $5 million study, were published last year. According to one of its midrange projections, annual global energy production will increase by 80% by 2020, to the equivalent of 16 billion metric tons of oil. That output will be needed to meet the needs of a human population that will be on its way from 5.5 billion (the 1990 figure) to 8.1 billion in 2020. (The numbers come from estimates by the United Nations and the World Bank.)

The American Wind Energy Association (Washington, DC) foresees 10,000 MW of wind generation in the United States by 2000, five times that by 2010, and an eventual takeover of 20% of U.S. power generation.

The U.S. Department of Commerce forecasts the world market for small-scale and intermediate-scale utility-interconnect wind turbines to grow at double- or even triple-digit rates. If performance-based tax credits and production payments are enacted in the United States, similar dramatic growth is forecast for the domestic market. With increased use of these turbines in the Asia-Pacific region, the number of U.S.-produced small-scale turbines sold is expected to double every two years during the 1995 to 1999 period.

The grid-connected PV market is expected to be very large, but the big question is when. Timing is dependent on market factors, including the cost of conventional energy, the cost of PV systems (not just modules), utility acceptance of PV systems, and regulatory controls. Each of these factors will have a major impact on the demand for PV.

The fact that a low cost storage device (e.g. battery) does not exist often significantly decreases the value of PV for a utility (summer peak loads often last until 10 p.m.). Utilities have little or no incentive to take risks. They are intimately familiar with conventional generating sources and receive no rewards for taking risks with new technologies. Nuclear power plants have embarrassed many utilities, some of which are still near bankruptcy. They will not gamble on another new technology (PV) without a decade or two of evaluation and/or strong incentives which are yet undefined.

According to World Information Technologies, Inc. (Northport, NY), the U.S. photovoltaic industry is expected to outpace world PV module shipments growth during the 1990s. U.S. shipments are forecast to reach 240 MW by 2000, or 35% of the global market. Higher world energy prices, growing energy needs in developing countries, and the large share of the Third World population living in remote villages will favor U.S. solar cell and module exports, which are forecast to reach 99 MW during 2000, or 44% of domestic market sales. PV demand will continue to increase among electric utilities and other industrial users through increased government funding, complimented by the growing worldwide interest in an inexhaustible and clean energy source to solve many of the worlds environmental problems. This could boost worldwide demand to 681 MW by 2000, as shipments increase at a 29% annual average compound rate between 1995 and 2000.

In late 1997, the Northwest's first geothermal project will become operational. A 30 MW pilot project by Bonneville Power Administration will provide enough electricity to serve approximately 30,000 households. Geothermal power is considered one of the most promising resources for meeting the 21st century's power needs.

M-C Power Corporation plans to introduce the first commercial molten-carbonate fuel cell power plants in 1998. The MW-class skid-mounted system operates on natural gas.

Both the near and longer-term outlook for the U.S. geothermal industry point to an acceleration in the rate of growth of additional geothermal power output capacity installed in new or existing plants. Most, if not all, of this growth will be driven by private power project development. As a result, the division of ownership of installed geothermal power capacity in the United States will be reversed by the end of the 1990s, with almost 60% of cumulative geothermal capacity installed by that time located on independently owned private power plants, and 40% on utility-owned plants.

17.5 Opportunities

One of the biggest unknowns driving the renewable energy market is regulatory factors which may impact a utility's generation mix and the cost of conventional energy generation. The public and Congress have been slow in responding to environmental concerns; however sensitivity and concern appear to be rising at a rapid rate. If the cost of externalities (e.g. environmental damage) were included in the cost of power generation, generation costs could double overnight. Little is expected to happen quickly with regulatory factors until the cost of oil increases or the public becomes more concerned about the environment.

18 ENVIRONMENTAL ISSUES AND POLLUTION CONTROL

CONTENTS:

18.1 Trends and Market Assessment
18.2 Recent Activities
18.3 Short Term Outlook
18.4 Mid-Range and Long Term Outlook
18.5 Opportunities

18.1 Trends and Market Assessment

Electric utilities face several strong environmental challenges:

- Air pollution control
- Electric and magnetic field exposure
- Water pollution control
- Greenhouse gas emissions

The Clean Air Act Amendments of 1990 have had a major impact on electric utilities. By 2000, annual SO_2 emissions will be cut to about nine million tons. This is less than half of the 1980 level of 19 million tons. The clean air program will be implemented in two phases:

- Phase I: Takes effect in 1995 and requires the 110 most pollution-intensive power plants, located in 21 states, to reduce their total SO_2 emissions to approximately 60% of their aggregate 1980 level.

- Phase II: Becomes effective in 2000 and affects about 800, less pollution-intensive plants. Phase II cuts total annual SO_2 emissions to less than half the 1980 level.

According to Future Technology Surveys, Inc. (Lilburn, GA), the potential liability to electric utilities relating to electric and magnetic field (EMF) exposure is $20 billion. The greatest liability would be related to increased right-of-way purchases and litigation.

The 15 or so EMF studies completed since the late 1970s have drawn various conclusions about possible links between EMF and some types of cancer, but none have identified a definite association between the forces and any one type.

In 1993, the utility industry spent more than $11 million on electric and magnetic field research through the Electric Power Research Institute. According to Edison Electric Institute, utilities have contributed nearly $80 million to EMF research since the early 1970s.

Electric utilities use huge amounts of water, 68 trillion gallons annually (187 billion gallons per day), most of it for condenser and reactor cooling. Steam electric power plants use approximately 47% of the water intake in the United States.

There is a modest decline in water withdrawals by utilities on an annual basis as more recycle and reuse (zero discharge) is implemented. The primary reason for this trend is the increasing cost of water. The most common method of reuse is the installation of cooling towers.

According to William T. Lorenz & Company (Janesville, WI), the 1993 electric utility expenditures on water treatment were $720 million. Expenditures on wastewater treatment in 1993 were $962 million. The combined water and wastewater expenditures of $1.68 billion were distributed as follows:

- Design/Engineering: $105 million
- Equipment: $393 million

- Instruments: $46 million
- Construction: $1.138 billion

The major portion of wastewater treatment expenditures have been for end-of-line treatment, with approximately 20% of expenditures going for in-process changes.

On Earth Day, 22 April 1993, President Clinton announced the Climate Change Action Package, a new commitment to return U.S. greenhouse gas emissions to their 1990 levels by 2000. Current estimates show that between 70 million and 100 million metric tons of additional carbon-equivalent emissions reductions are necessary to attain this level. Immediately following the announcement of the Climate Change Action Package, the U.S. Department of Energy announced the Climate Change Partnership. Initially, 61 of the largest utilities, responsible for more than 60% of utility carbon emissions, volunteered to participate in the program. The agreement outlines options utilities can use under the Energy Policy Act of 1992, including fuel-switching to lower-carbon fuels, methane capture, forestry carbon sequestration, energy efficiency, more efficient fleets, and international reduction programs.

The issue of global warming has loomed as a potential blockbuster for electric utilities for several years. In the extreme, there could be legislation calling for a phaseout of fossil fuel generation.

Numerous state public utility commissions are developing procedures for explicitly incorporating environmental costs, or externalities, into the integrated resource planning (IRP) process. New offerings for non-utility generation and heightened demands by ratepayers and regulators for environmentally safe sources of power are steering externality review to the forefront as both a policy and ratemaking issue in future energy decisions. Companies planning to supply new power capacity in at least 18 states, and potentially 26 others, will face new programs to include externality costs in power pricing. In some of these states, regulators require utilities to internalize the environment costs of all resource options, but do not specify the methods to be used. Other states, including California, Massachusetts, Nevada, New Jersey, New York, Oregon, Vermont, and Wisconsin, have prescribed specific quantitative measures. In Nevada, for example, environmental costs are added to plant construction and operating costs, and purchased power costs to determine the true "societal" cost of the project.

18.2 Recent Activities

In February 1994, *Electric Light & Power* reported the risks associated with electric and magnetic fields (EMF) top the list of utility executive concerns. This concern is well founded. A recent article in the American Bar Association Journal suggests that EMF litigation "exhibits significant parallels to asbestos litigation at a similar stage in its development."

To date, the utility industry has been successful in defending EMF actions. In May 1994, Georgia Power successfully defended litigation that a woman's non-Hodgkin's lymphoma was not caused by her exposure to EMF from power lines. Similarly, a jury rejected the claim against San Diego Gas & Electric (SDG&E) that a girl's kidney tumor resulted from her exposure to EMF. It was reported that SDG&E spent more than $2 million in defense legal fees.

A study of EMF exposures to 223,000 employees of Hydro-Quebec, Ontario and Electricite de France was published in 1994. It was the largest EMF study to date, and found no "definitive evidence" of a link between EMFs and cancer among utility workers.

In 1994, the U.S. Department of Energy budgeted $4 million to start a five-year national EMF research program, as mandated under the Energy Policy Act of 1992. Utilities and equipment manufacturers are expected to contribute matching funds.

According to The McIlvaine Company (Northbrook, IL), the U.S. power industry spend $1.326 billion on air pollution control in 1994. This represented about 36% of total U.S. expenditures.

Electric utilities completed implementation in 1994 with the Phase I requirements of the Clean Air Act of 1990 to meet the 01 January 1995 compliance date. The methods of compliance with the Phase I requirements were identified by the Energy Information Administration. Of the 261 electric generating units at 110 power plant locations, 62% will achieve Phase I compliance by switching to, or blending with low-sulfur coals, or by cofiring with other fuels (usually natural gas). Switching is popular with utilities because of the low costs of low-sulfur coals and the smaller capital expenditures involved with the change than with other emissions-reduction options. Approximately 10% of the 261 units will utilize flue gas desulfurization systems (FGD). However, these scrubber systems, while seemingly small in number, will account for more than 16% of the overall emissions reduction. Electric utilities plan to meet CAAA requirements for 15% of the units with clean air allowances bought from others. In addition, approximately 10% of the 261 units already are in compliance, about 3% will be retired, and at least one unit will be repowered. Costs associated with changes planned to bring units into compliance vary widely. For six selected utilities, the costs ranged from $2.60 per kW to $17.20 kW (1993 dollars).

A separate compliance study was completed by Industrial Information Services (Reno, NV). According to IIS, switching to lower-sulfur coal was the most popular strategy for SO_2 emissions control, for Phase I and Phase II compliance. Fifty-six percent of utilities with at least one unit subject to Phase I regulations will use this strategy to meet Phase I requirements, and 41% of coal-burning utilities plan to adopt this strategy for Phase II compliance. Eighty-two percent of utilities with at least one unit subject to Phase I regulations will install low NOx burners, and 82% of coal-burning utilities plan to install low NOx burners to meet Phase II regulations.

The second annual sulphur dioxide (SO_2) allowance auction was held in 1994 at the Chicago Board of Trade. More allowances were sold than in 1993 (175,200 vs. 150,010); the average price climbed slightly, to $152 per allowance; and auction bids were clustered more tightly around the average. Allowance Holding Corporation bought about 70% of the allowances sold at the 1994 auction with two electric utilities, American Municipal Power (Ohio) and Tampa Electric, buying most of the remainder. Carolina Power & Light and Duke Power Company were the major buyers at the 1993 auction.

The first trading of nitrogen oxide (NOx) credits occurred on 11 March 1994, when Public Service Electric & Gas Company announced the sale of 100 NOx emission credits annually for five years to Northeast Utilities.

On 18 November 1994, Niagara Mohawk Power Corporation exchanged 1.75 million CO_2 allowances for 25,000 SO_2 allowances from Arizona Public Service Company It was the first exchange of its kind.

On 27 September 1994, ten of the twelve member states in the Ozone Transport Commission and the District of Columbia announced an agreement for reduction of NOx emissions by up to 65% over five years, and by 75% by May 2003. ICF Kaiser International estimates capital expenditures of $1 billion to $2 billion by the end of the decade and annual costs between $266 million and $436 million to achieve the 75% goal. Virginia and Massachusetts abstained from the pact.

On 29 November 1994, the U.S. Court of Appeals remanded EPA's requirement for implementation of overfire control technology to control NOx emissions. The ruling stated that EPA exceeded its statutory authority by not also allowing Low-NOx burners or other technologies to meet emission goals. Utilities had been facing a 01 January 1995 deadline prior to the ruling.

Earth Day 1994 brought more utility commitments for carbon dioxide reduction to Washington, under the Department of Energy's Climate Challenge plan. Major utility groups representing hundreds of investor-owned, municipal, and rural electric utilities pledged to CO_2 reductions in the voluntary effort to help cut suspected greenhouse gas emissions to 1990 levels by 2000. Public Service Electric & Gas Company (Newark, NJ) was the first to join the initiative. PSE&G's emission reduction measures will include repowering of older electric plants with gas-fired combined-cycle turbines, demand-side management and conservation projects, seasonal fuel switching at generation stations, new emissions control technology and promoting natural gas vehicles.

18.3 Short Term Outlook

The electric utility industry's continued success in defending EMF actions is by no means assured, according to Francis A. Citera (Pope, Cahill & Devine). More litigation is a virtual certainty in 1995. The industry must be prepared to vigorously defend such actions. A single loss at trial will most assuredly open a floodgate of litigation, much as it did for asbestos, and set the stage for a future class action.

Some important environmental legislation is expected to be reauthorized in 1995. Clean Water Act reauthorization may limit the use of water from rivers, lakes, streams, etc., for cooling. The Gulf of Mexico is currently being considered for special rules which may require treatment of all water put into waterways feeding into the Gulf (even rain water runoff) and stop or limit the use of river water for cooling applications. The Great Lakes Initiative (a special program for the Great Lakes) is reportedly leading to several plant closings and economic consequences for the Midwest.

According to The McIlvaine Company (Northbrook, IL), the U.S. power industry will spend $1.591 billion on air pollution control in 1995. This is a 17% increase over 1994 expenditures.

18.4 Mid-Range and Long Term Outlook

Retail wheeling may have an influence on pollution control. Proponents of retail wheeling suggest that load lost to retail wheeling will reduce pollution from utility sources. The efficiency of new generation would pollute less than older utility generation sources.

A potential $41 billion expenditure for cooling tower construction looms for electric utilities if a variance provision of the Clean Water Act is repealed. Under the Clean Water Act, some utilities are allowed to discharge the water from the steam plants if they can show that the effluent does not upset the balance of the fish and wildlife population at the discharge site. A bill was proposed by the Senate Committee on Environment and Public Works to repeal the variances. According to an EEI-sponsored study by Stone & Webster Engineering Corporation (Boston, MA), adding cooling towers to the 679 U.S. powerplants that lack them to avoid discharges of heated water could cost more than $41 billion. The potentially affected powerplants produce about 32% of U.S. steam generating capacity.

18.5 Opportunities

New ways of reducing nitrogen-oxide emissions were discussed at the 1994 ASME-sponsored International Joint Power Generation Conference. Solutions ranged from a multi-annular burner design from the Massachusetts Institute of Technology to a gas reburning process cited by Energy & Environmental Research Corporation (Irvine, CA). A 70% reduction was claimed for reburning, an injection process that involves refitting the boilers and altering combustion staging in a coal-fired facility.

19 ELECTRIC VEHICLES

CONTENTS:

19.1 Trends and Market Assessment
19.2 Recent Activities
19.3 Short Term Outlook
19.4 Mid-Range and Long Term Outlook
19.5 Opportunities

19.1 Trends and Market Assessment

Clean air requirements, both federal and state, are the driving force behind the development of alternative fuel vehicles, which include ethanol, methanol, electric vehicles, natural gas, and hydrogen.

The federal Clean Air Act Amendments of 1990 provided a dual set of motor vehicle emission standards, one for California and one for the remaining 49 states. The California low-emission vehicle standards require that 2% of all light vehicles (automobiles, and light trucks and vans with loaded weight of 3,750 pounds or less) sold in the state be zero-emission vehicles (ZEVs), beginning in 1998. The quota increases to 5% in 2001 and 10% in 2003. Current technology practically mandates these ZEVs be battery-powered electric vehicles. EPA ruled in 1992 that other states may adopt the more stringent California regulations as an alternative to the federal standards. Therefore, beginning in 1998, production model electric vehicles (EVs) will be sold in other states that have either adopted, or are expected to adopt, the California regulations. With the exception of Florida, EV demand in states where their use is not mandated is expected to remain negligible.

As of January 1994, estimates show that approximately $1 billion had been spent on electric vehicle development.

19.2 Recent Activities

Electric vehicle batteries advanced on several fronts recently. These include:

- $32.9 million in funding from the U.S. Advanced Battery Consortium for an advanced lithium-polymer battery technology, the largest award given to date. The U.S. Advanced Battery Consortium was recently formed and includes the U.S. Department of Energy, the Electric Power Research Institute, General Motors, Ford, and Chrysler.

- 30-month testing of the ABB sodium-sulfur battery in 105 Ford Ecostar vehicles

- Development of a quick-change battery system for use with electric-vehicle (EV) pickup trucks.

The testing of nine electric vehicles from five manufacturers in Phoenix in late 1994 demonstrated some technological barriers which are being overcome in EV technology. The tests were sponsored by the U.S. Department of Energy, and comparison was made with specifications developed by EV America. Highlights of the test results include:

- Five of the vehicles achieved maximum speeds of 70 mph or greater.

- Four of the vehicles achieved ranges of 70 miles or more at a constant speed of 45 mph on the track.

- All of the vehicles showed stability during the braking test.

- A charge time of less than four hours was achieved by one of the vehicles at 208 or 240 volts.

- None of the vehicles were able to meet the acceleration goals stated in EV America specifications.

- Several of the vehicles outperformed their gasoline-powered counterparts in the road-handling test.

The Arizona Public Service Electric 500, a 125-mile race for electric vehicles, was held in March 1994.

The electric vehicle national speed record of 183 mph was set on 11 March 1994 by a General Motors Impact electric vehicle at the Fort Stockton (Texas) Test Center.

The 1994 goal was for 7,500 alternative-fueled vehicles be added to the federal fleet. The number of electric vehicles purchased is not known, but probably was a very small part of the mix. Federal agencies requested 5,520 alternative-fueled vehicles for 1993: 2,865 fueled by alcohol, 2,652 natural gas-fueled vehicles, and only three electric vehicles.

19.3 Short Term Outlook

There will be increased activity to develop and promote EV technology among utilities in 1995. A national initiative, known as *EV America*, was formed by 14 electric utilities across the nation to work together on a multi-phased demonstration of electric vehicles by the end of 1997. The goal is to place 5,000 electric vehicles into utility, commercial, government, and/or transit fleet application.

A closely watched development in 1995 will be legislation requiring the introduction of commercial EVs in California beginning in 1998. The obstacle making this requirement practical is lack of state-of-the-art battery technology. Robert Smock, editorial director for *Power Engineering*, calls the inability to develop a better storage battery "one major technological development failure in the 20th century." The Big Three automakers seem to have made a strong case for California to postpone its legislation. "Who, they asked, will want to buy a car with a half-ton gas tank that holds the equivalent of two gallons of gas? Such a car would cost $35,000 and require an eight hour recharge every 100 miles. No one, said the automakers, will buy a lemon like that." So far, the California legislators have not backed down.

In the spring of 1995, Blue Bird (Macon, GA) will deliver the first heavy-duty electric school bus to Antelope Valley Schools Transportation Agency (Lancaster, PA).

The acquisition targets set by U.S. Department of Energy for the purchase of alternative-fueled vehicles by federal agencies is 10,000 in 1995

19.4 Mid-Range and Long Term Outlook

The obvious market driver for the EV market is air pollution regulations. However, there are two other strong potentials driving the development of a large EV market:

- Electric vehicle costs may decrease to the point where the purchase price becomes lower than internal combustion automobiles.

- Electric utilities make use of electric vehicles attractive through leasing programs, convenient billing, shared-savings,or other programs.

A scenario suggested by the Electric Power Research Institute (Palo Alto, CA) shows a gradual shift toward EVs in many different commercial markets, beginning with van fleets and expanding to light trucks and passenger cars used for short-range driving. EPRI's considering other electric transportation alternatives, such as hybrids (combining EV batteries and internal combustion engines in the same vehicles) and different types of mass transit systems, for their potential role in a shift away from burning gasoline in the approximately 150 million vehicles in use in America. EPRI studies, based on an average electricity use of 30 kWh/day per vehicle, show a nationwide distribution of just two million EVs producing an annual electricity demand of 21.94×10^9 kWh. If these figures are applied to Electric Vehicle Development Corporation's most conservative estimates of market growth, utilities will earn some $35 billion from EVs between 1990 and 2010 with virtually no new capacity required.

Georgia Power Company's CEO, A.W. Dahlberg, would like to see a significant number of electric vehicles in Atlanta by 2000. In an interview with Atlanta Business Chronicle, Dahlberg predicted that electric vehicles will make a significant difference in Georgia Power's earnings. While Georgia Power's earnings are respectable, future markets did not seem as promising. Sales are growing at only 2.2% to 2.5% per year. Dahlberg examined Georgia Power's markets and transportation stood out as a good potential growth possibility.

The goal of the United States Advanced Battery Consortium is to make electric vehicles competitive by 2000. The consortium, which includes General Motors, Chrysler, Ford Motor Company, and the Electric Power Research Institute, was founded in 1991 as a $260 million public-private venture to develop batteries for electric vehicles. The U.S. Department of Energy evenly splits the cost of the project, because "the development of a competitive electronic auto industry would do more to reduce oil imports than rigid fuel efficiency standards."

In Japan, MITI's Agency of Industrial Science and Technology launched a $108 million, ten year development project in electric vehicle technology. Research began in 1993.

Based on standards established by the U.S. Department of Energy, in 1996, 25% of each federal agency's acquisition must be alternative-fueled vehicles, rising to 33% in 1997 and 50% in 1998.

The Freedonia Group (Cleveland, OH) forecasts demand for electric vehicles in the U.S. reaching 155,000 units in 1998 and 845,000 units in 2003. Prior to 1998, electric vehicle demand will be negligible and limited to prototype and market niche models. Environmental regulations will be the primary driving force for electric vehicle demand.

The Sacramento Municipal Utility District intends to make Sacramento, Calif. the "clean air capital of the nation" by 2005. To achieve this goal, SMUD is actively promoting the widespread use of electricity as a replacement for petroleum in all forms of transportation while generating electricity with a minimum impact on air quality. Specifically, this entails the promotion of electric vehicle development and commercialization within the Sacramento area. SMUD's plans also call for expanding Sacramento's Regional Transit (RT) electric transit systems and construction of a high speed inter-city electric rail service from the Sacramento area.

19.5 Opportunities

From the perspective of the electric utility, EVs are one of the major new markets for electricity. In addition, since they can be recharged at off-peak times, EVs can increase a utility's revenues and help with load management while requiring little or no capital investment. Increased demand for off-peak electricity will lead to lower average electricity costs for both commercial and residential utility customers. EVs also offer electric utilities new business opportunities in local EV sales and service. Battery leasing is another promising business opportunity resulting from the EV infrastructure; many EV owners will opt to lease instead of buy propulsion batteries, decreasing the initial cost of the vehicles. In the future, the role of electric utilities may include promotion and leasing, sales, service, maintenance, drive-train service, and battery leasing/service.

The Energy Policy Act of 1992 (EPAct) contains authorization for more than $500 million in federal programs to assist industry in research and development areas as well as in the commercial demonstration of vehicles and the deployment of infrastructure support systems for those vehicles. In addition, there are incentives for the use of electric vehicles under the fleet requirements of the EPAct, and EPAct provides very important tax incentives for both vehicles and infrastructure. Specifically, EPAct created a tax credit for business and individual purchasers of electric vehicles. The tax credit is equal to 10% of the purchase price of an electric vehicle, up to a maximum credit of $4,000. The act also creates a $100,000 tax deduction per refueling site for businesses that install alternative fuel refueling property, including property used in recharging electric vehicles. Both of these tax incentives became available July 1, 1993 and will continue to be available until after 2000. In addition, EPAct authorizes a 10 year, $50 million electric vehicle commercial demonstration program to accelerate development and use of electric vehicles as well as a five year, $40 million federal government/private industry cooperative program to research, develop, and demonstrate electric vehicles infrastructure. An incentive program is also authorized to support sales, in an effort to introduce alternatively fueled vehicles. The legislation also imposes mandatory requirements for the acquisition of alternatively fueled vehicles on federal fleets, state government fleets, and fleets operated by the providers of alternative fuels.

20 RATES

CONTENTS:

20.1 Trends and Market Assessment
20.2 Recent Activities
20.3 Short Term Outlook
20.4 Mid-Range and Long Term Outlook
20.5 Opportunities

20.1 Trends and Market Assessment

According to the U.S. Department of Energy, the average end-use price of electricity for all sectors in the United States was $0.068 per kilowatt hour in 1992, down from $0.071 in 1990. The end-use price by sector in 1992 was:

- Residential: $0.081 per kilowatt hour
- Commercial: $0.075 per kilowatt hour
- Industrial: $0.051 per kilowatt hour
- Transportation: $0.051 per kilowatt hour

20.2 Recent Activities

In July 1994, the average electricity price to industrial customers by 170 U.S. electric utilities was $0.047 per kWh. The highest rate was $0.146 per kWh from Consolidated Edison, and the lowest was $0.0171 kWh from Ohio Valley Electric. These figures are based on DoE Form EIA-826 and a survey by *Energy User News* and were obtained by dividing total revenue by total kWh sold to industrial customers.

Based on the same sources, the average electricity price to commercial customers by utilities in June 1994 was about $0.072 per kWh. The highest rate was $0.1564 per kWh from Hawaii Electric Light Company, and the lowest was $0.0323 from Seattle City Light Company.

In early 1994, the Federal Energy Regulatory Commission announced their adoption of a new policy on incentive rates for regulated electric utilities, defined by FERC as rate structures intended to encourage utilities to operate more efficiently. FERC has found that "traditional cost-of-service regulations lack the mechanisms that foster efficiency." FERC will attempt to encourage long-term efficiency improvements through its ratemaking by divorcing rates from cost-of-service, lengthening the time between rate cases, and, most importantly, "sharing the benefits of cost savings between consumers and stockholders."

The major FERC ruling relating to rates in 1994 was the decision overturning the Connecticut law requiring electric utilities to purchase electricity by a resource recovery facility owned or operated by or for the benefit of a municipality at the same rate that the electric utility charges the municipality for electricity. FERC ruled the utility may not be required to pay greater than avoided costs for power from a resource recovery facility.

20.3 Short Term Outlook

Based on Form EIA-861 responses by investor-owned utilities, the Energy Information Administration developed projections for electricity rates. The EIA projections show essentially no growth in real electricity price through 1997, and inflation averaging 2.6% per year.

20.4 Mid-Range and Long Term Outlook

In the *Annual Energy Outlook 1994*, the Energy Information Administration of the U.S. Department of Energy makes the following forecasts for the average end-use price of electricity in 2000:

- High economic growth:
  - Residential: $0.088 per kilowatt hour
  - Commercial: $0.078 per kilowatt hour
  - Industrial: $0.052 per kilowatt hour
  - Average for all sectors: $0.071 per kilowatt hour

- Low economic growth:
  - Residential: $0.085 per kilowatt hour
  - Commercial: $0.075 per kilowatt hour
  - Industrial: $0.050 per kilowatt hour
  - Average for all sectors: $0.069 per kilowatt hour

Forecasts for electricity rates in 2000 by other groups are (average for all sectors):

- Edison Electric Institute: $0.071 per kilowatt hour
- Gas Research Institute: $0.0635 per kilowatt hour
- The WEFA Group: $0.0733 per kilowatt hour
- DRI/McGraw-Hill: $0.065 per kilowatt hour

The following cost forecast is made by EIA for 2010:

- High economic growth:
  - Residential: $0.103 per kilowatt hour
  - Commercial: $0.084 per kilowatt hour
  - Industrial: $0.057 per kilowatt hour
  - Average for all sectors: $0.079 per kilowatt hour

- Low economic growth:
  - Residential: $0.092 per kilowatt hour
  - Commercial: $0.077 per kilowatt hour
  - Industrial: $0.052 per kilowatt hour
  - Average for all sectors: $0.072 per kilowatt hour

Forecasts for electricity rates in 2010 by other groups are (average for all sectors):

- Edison Electric Institute: $0.0718 per kilowatt hour
- Gas Research Institute: $0.0618 per kilowatt hour
- The WEFA Group: $0.0801 per kilowatt hour
- DRI/McGraw-Hill: $0.065 per kilowatt hour

The GRI and DRI price projections are lower than EIA's because of lower fuel prices to the electricity sector. WEFA's prices are higher and slightly above EIA's high growth rate case.

20.5 Opportunities

According to Arthur Andersen & Company (New York, NY) and Cambridge Energy Research Associates, Inc. (Cambridge, MA), some aspects of the "just another commodity" revolution that has overtaken other sectors of the U.S. energy supply industry seem certain to spill over into the electric utility business. The most obvious is the growing financial strength and operational flexibility of the truly low-cost producer. Assuming that restrictions of transmission access are removed by the end of the decade, there could be a class of low-cost electricity suppliers in the power industry. This will include a mixture of both traditional utilities and NUGs, and include the companies that have adopted best practices in cost-containment policies.

Utility ratemaking will need to change with respect to increased reliance upon purchased power from other wholesale generation sources. This will include the necessity of reviewing opportunities permitting electric utilities to earn a rate of return on prudent and cost effective power purchases, particularly structured and priced at levels less than the more accurate and posted avoided costs. This will create certain economies and efficiencies to negotiate and secure power purchase contracts at less than posted avoided cost rates resulting in a sharing of those benefits directly with the electric utilities, ratepayers, and its shareholders. This approach would start addressing the theoretical concerns regarding the risks of power purchasing recently advanced by the ratings agencies which really mask fundamental concerns with regulatory uncertainty in such purchases. These uncertainties are no different than fuel contracting by utilities, utility power purchases from other utilities, or uncertainties with the utility's own construction program.

REFERENCES

Chapter 1

"Energy for Tomorrow's World," United States Energy Association, Washington, DC, 1994.

Falcone, C.A., "Retail Wheeling: The Sword of Damocles," Wheeling & Transmission Monthly, September 1994, p. 1.

"Regulatory and Legislative Precedents," Demand-Side Monthly, May 1994, p. 9.

Smith, D.J., "1996 is Expected to be a Watershed Year for the U.S. Electric Industry," Power Engineering, October 1994, p. 12.

Weiss, L., "FERC Looks Beyond EPAct," Wheeling & Transmission Monthly, January 1995, p. 1.

Chapter 2

"APPA Meeting Focuses on New Competition," Electric Light & Power, September 1994, p. 20.

Daniels, Stephen H., and Allen Soast, "Design Firms Shaken by Utility Deregulation," Engineering News Record, April 11, 1994, p. 8-9.

Dreilinger, C., "Deregulation Driving Utilities to Change," Electric Light & Power, December 1994, p. 3.

Falcone, C.A., "Retail Wheeling: The Sword of Damocles," Wheeling & Transmission Monthly, September 1994, p. 1.

Feldman, R.D., "Time to Hedge Your Bets," Cogeneration Monthly Letter, January 1995, p. 1.

"FERC Sets Rules for Affiliated Power Marketers," Wheeling & Transmission Monthly," October 1994, p. 1.

"Northeast Utilities, Client to Pay a Power Supplier," Wall Street Journal, 18 May 1994, p. A4.

Reardon, R.E., "Planned Expenditures Down Sharply," Electric Light & Power, December 1994, p. 37.

R.J. Rudden Associates, Fitch Investors Service, "Electric Utility Competition: What do Regulators Say?" Cogeneration and Competitive Power Journal, Spring 1994, p. 7-16.

Weiss, L., "FERC Looks Beyond EPAct," Wheeling & Transmission Monthly, January 1995, p. 1.

Zimmer, M.J., and P.G. Lookadoo, "Will Power Marketing Parallel Gas Marketing?" Cogeneration and Competitive Power Journal, Fall 1994, p. 56-60.

Zimmer, M.J., "New Energy Policy Act Prospects for Change," Cogeneration and Competitive Power Journal, v 8, n 2, 1993, p. 14.

Chapter 3

"AEP: Stranded Investment Denied," Cogeneration Monthly Letter, July 1994, p. 1.

"Commission Proposes Rule for Recovery of Stranded Costs," World Cogeneration, September/October 1994, p. 3.

"EGA Supports Recovery of Stranded Costs," The Cogeneration Monthly Letter, December 1994, p. 1.

"FERC Seeks to Spread the Pain," Cogeneration Monthly Letter, July 1994, p. 1.

Hocker, C., "Invoking New Strategies," Independent Energy, October 1993, p. 26.

Hoske, M.T., "Investor-Owned 100 Utilities, Top 100 1993 Financial Performances," Electric Light & Power, June 1993, p. 11.

Hoske, M., "Net Income Falls Despite Higher Sales for Investor-Owned Utilities in 1993," Electric Light & Power, June 1994, p. 11.

"IOUs Step Up Nonutility Business Ventures," Electric Light & Power, November 1994, p. 3.

"Longer Life," Energy User News, 23 January 1995, p. 22.

"New Proposal For Stranded Cost," Wheeling & Transmission Monthly, July 1994, p. 1.

Stein, H., "Systems Integration/Outsourcing will Triple," Electric Light & Power, August 1994, p. 6.

"Utilities Approve Merger," Electric Light & Power, December 1994, p. 6.

"Utilities Merge for Cost Savings," Electric Light & Power, February 1994, p. 1.

"Utilities Urged to Enter Race on Info Highway," Electric Light & Power, March 1994, p. 1.

Warkentin, D., "Utility Liable for Power Quality," Electric Light & Power, September 1994, p. 1.

Warkentin, D., "Electricity Forum Examines New Game Plan for Power Industry," Electric Light & Power, January 1995, p. 1.

Chapter 4

Anderson, J. and M.T. Burr, "Progressive Change," Independent Energy, November 1994, p. 10.

Daniels, Stephen H., and Allen Soast, "Design Firms Shaken by Utility Deregulation," Engineering News Record, April 11, 1994, p. 8-9.

"Development of the Independent Power Industry," Power Engineering, May 1994, p. 26.

Dickenson, Ronald L., Alan Karp, and Dale R. Simbeck, "Comparing the Alternatives," Independent Energy, November 1993, p. 60.

Donnelly, A.T., "Washington State Utility District Selects Diverse Packages of Diverse Independent Power Resources," World Cogeneration, November/December 1994, p. 16.

Hoffman, Scott L., "Financing Non-Utility Power Projects," Cogeneration and Competitive Power Journal, Fall 1994, p. 36-42.

"Independents Take 'Exempt Wholesale Generator' Route," Power Engineering, May 1994, p. 7.

"New Generating Capacity Plans Depend on Utility IRPs," Electric Light & Power, May 1994, p. 10.

"New Venture Proposes Projects in Northwest," Engineering News Record, February 28, 1994, p. 25-26.

Pender, R.B., "Decade of Change Begins for the Maturing Independent Energy Industry," Cogeneration Journal, Spring 1991, p. 8.

"PG&E/Bechtel Partnership to Acquire J. Makowski Company," The Cogeneration Monthly Letter, August 1994, p. 3.

"Profile of the U.S. Independent Power Market: 1994 Status and Trends," RCG/Hagler Bailly, Inc., Arlington, VA, 1994.

Tessmer, R.G., "Markets for Wheeling Cogenerated Power," Cogen, Winter 1994, p. 8.

"U.S. Firm Scoring Big in China's Power Play," Engineering News Record, September 19, 1994, p 26.

Chapter 5

Annual Energy Outlook 1994, Energy Information Administration, 1994.

Annual Energy Review 1993, Energy Information Administration, 1994.

Annual Electric Utility Report, U.S. Department of Energy, Form EIA-861.

"Electric Energy Demand Expected to Increase," Electric Light & Power, November 1994, p. 4.

"New York Power Authority Cancels $5-Billion Hydro-Quebec Power Contract," Electric Light & Power, June 1994, p. 1.

"Regulatory and Legislative Precedents," Demand-Side Monthly, May 1994, p. 9.

Chapter 6

Parkinson, G., "Free Wheeling in a Deregulated Market," Chemical Engineering, January 1995, p. 29.

Selgrade, E.L., "Wholesale Ratemaking for EWGs," Proceedings of the 1993 World Energy Engineering Congress, p. 573.

Zimmer, M.J., "New Energy Policy Act Prospects for Change," Cogeneration and Competitive Power Journal, v 8, n 2, 1993, p. 14.

Chapter 7

Anderson, J.L. and M.T. Burr, "Progressive Change," International Energy, November 1994, p. 10.

"California Pushes Restructuring," Retail Wheeling," May 15, 1994, p. 10.

"Connecticut Rejects Retail Wheeling," Electric Light & Power, November 1994, p. 1.

Dykhuis, P.E. and L. Weiss, "The Michigan Retail Wheeling Experiment," Cogen Magazine, Spring 1994, p. 17.

Falcone, C.A., "Retail Wheeling: The Sword of Damocles," Wheeling & Transmission Monthly, September 1994, p. 1.

Gahran, A., "Big 3 to Forego Cogeneration, Wheeling for 10 Years," Energy User News, October 1994, p. 1.

"Group Calls for Retail Wheeling in Ohio," Electric Light & Power, January 1995, p. 6.

Hoske, M.T., "Retail Wheeling Quickens Reform," Electric Light & Power, June 1994, p. 3.

Maremont, M., "Shock Treatment for California Utilities," Business Week, 09 May 1994, p. 32.

Olson, R.A., "Connecticut: Commission Rules on Retail Wheeling," The Cogeneration Monthly Letter, November 1994, p. 8.

Olson, R.A., "Pennsylvania: Utilities Claim Retail Wheeling will Cost $10 Billion in Stranded Investment," The Cogeneration Monthly Letter, December 1994, p. 8.

Parkinson, G., "Free Wheeling in a Deregulated Market," Chemical Engineering, January 1995, p. 29.

"Retail Wheeling not in Immediate Future, Panel Says," Electric Light & Power, January 1995, p. 6.

"Retail Wheeling Risky for Pennsylvania," Electric Light & Power, December 1994, p. 10.

"Retail Wheeling to Begin in Calif., Mich.," Electric Light & Power, July 1994, p. 1.

Smock, B., "Speeding Down the Free Market Highway," Electric Light & Power, September 1994, p. 5.

"State Pushes Competition," Engineering News Record, November 28, 1994, p 14.

Tessmer, R.G., "Markets for Wheeling Cogenerated Power," Cogen, Winter 1994, p. 8.

"Transmission Price Flexibility Addressed in FERC Policy," Electric Light & Power, January 1995, p. 1.

"University of Missouri Runs Nation's First Retail Competitive Bid," Wheeling & Transmission Monthly, October 1994, p. 3.

"Vermont Questions Retail Wheeling," Fortnightly, May 15, 1994, p. 43.

Warkentin, D., "Retail Wheeling Packed with Possibilities," Electric Light & Power, p. 4.

Warkentin, D., "Wheeling Offers Savings Opportunities," Electric Light & Power, October 1994, p. 3.

"Washington State, Spurred by Big Industries, Eyes Retail Wheeling," Retail Power Monthly, January 1995, p. 6.

Chapter 8

Anderson, J. and M.T. Burr, "Progressive Change," Independent Energy, November 1994, p. 10.

Daniels, S.H., "Wind Power Finally Coming of Age," Engineering News Record, March 28, 1994, p. 8-9.

"Developers Score Big on Indonesia Projects," Engineering News Record, October 3, 1994, p 26.

"Electric Power Trends 1992," Cambridge Energy Research Associates and Arthur Andersen & Company, 1992.

Flanagan, R.T., "Italy Privatizes Energy," World Cogeneration, April/May 1994, p. 1.

Hoske, M.T., "T&D Conference Examines Global Competition," Electric Light & Power, June 1994, p. 1.

"Mexico Opens to Private Power," Engineering News Record, April 11, 1994, p 5.

Parkinson, G., "Free Wheeling in a Deregulated Market," Chemical Engineering, January 1995, p. 29.

"Power Market Heating Up in Vietnam," Engineering News Record, July 4, 1994, p 3.

"Private Power Market is Taking Off in India," Engineering News Record, October 3, 1994, p 16.

Roseman, E.J., "The Trillion Dollar Power Project Jackpot," Cogeneration and Competitive Power Journal, Spring 1994, p. 64-68.

Smith, S.G. and M. Buresch, "International Markets for Energy Efficiency Products and Services," Strategic Planning for Energy and the Environment, Summer 1994, p. 64-77.

Smock, R.W., "Prices Slashed 40% on New Pulverized Coal-Fired Power Plants," Power Engineering, November 1994, p. 23.

"The World Directory of New Electric Power Plants," UDI/McGraw-Hill, Washington, DC, 1994.

U.S. Agency for International Development, "Focus on South America," Cogeneration and Competitive Power Journal, Summer 1994, p. 35-37.

U.S. Agency for International Development, "MEXICO: A Complex Opportunity," Cogeneration and Competitive Power Journal, Spring 1994, p. 37-38.

Varrasi, J., "U.S. Power Industry Retrenches," World Cogeneration, November/December 1994, p. 11.

Zimmer, M.J., "New Energy Policy Act Prospects for Change," Cogeneration and Competitive Power Journal, v 8, n 2, 1993, p. 14.

Chapter 9

Annual Electric Utility Report, U.S. Department of Energy, Form EIA-861.

"BG&E Joins Ranks of DSM Rebate-Reducers," Strategies, Association of DSM Professionals, Fall 1994, p. 5.

"Detroit Edison Petitions PSC to Cut DSM Programs," Demand-Side Monthly, November 1994, p. 5.

"Demand-Side Management is too Valuable to Drop, nut its Future is Far from Secure," Electric Light & Power, April 1994, p. 6.

Duffy, G., "DSM: Its Programs, Problems, Potential," Engineered Systems, April 1993, p. 14.

"Electric Power Trends 1992," Cambridge Energy Research Associates and Arthur Andersen & Company, 1992.

"Entergy Reconciles DSM Rules with New Competitive Environment," Demand-Side Monthly, November 1994, p. 9.

Gahran, A., "Uncertainties Lead Utilities to Retreat from Rebates," Energy User News, November 1994, p. 1.

Goldman, C.A. and M.S. Kito, "Review of DSM Bidding Programs," Lawrence Berkeley Laboratory, 1994.

Hirst, E. and S. Hadley, "Price Impacts of Electric Utility DSM Programs," Oak Ridge National Laboratory, Report No. ORNL/CON-402, 1994.

Hocker, C., "The DSM Debate," Independent Energy, March 1993.

Hocker, C., "Invoking New Strategies," Independent Energy, October 1993, p. 26.

"Neglect DSM at Our Peril, Puget Power CEO Warns," Strategies, Association of DSM Professionals, Fall 1994, p. 9.

Meade, William and Elliot Roseman, "Make Room for DSM," Independent Energy 15, January 1992.

Moline, Barry, "Demand-Side Management in Public, the Quiet Revolution," Strategic Planning for Energy and the Environment, Vol. 12, No. 2, 1992, p. 54.

Nadel, S.M., and J.A. Jordan, "Industrial DSM Programs: What's Needed," Cogeneration and Competitive Power Journal, Summer 1994, p. 38-53.

"PECO Energy Proposes $10 million DSM Plan," Demand-Side Monthly, April 1994, p. 2.

"PG&E Feels Rates Pressure, DSM Impacted," Strategies, Association of DSM Professionals, Fall 1994, p. 5

Smock, R., "Retail Wheeling will Kill Utility Conservation Programs," Electric Light & Power, November 1994, p. 5.

Stein, H., "Demand-Side Management Programs Change Along with the Utility Industry," Electric Light & Power, January 1995, p. 17.

"Utility Rebate Programs Increase in Number but Change in Focus," Energy User News, May 1994, p. 16.

"Wall Street Analyst Sees General Decline in DSM," Strategies, Association of DSM Professionals, Fall 1994, p. 8.

"Will DSM Survive in a Competitive Power Market?" Demand-Side Monthly, August 1994, p. 2.

Wolcott, David R., "Second-Generation Demand-Side Management: A More Constructive Role for Performance Contracting Via ESCOs," Cogen and CompPower Journal, Vol. 8, No. 2, 1993.

"$4 Billion for DSM by '97 to Yield 74 TWh in Savings," Electric Light & Power, May 1994, p. 1.

Chapter 10

Bryant, F., "Big Turnout Expected Despite Absence of 'Big 4' Chiller Companies," Energy User News, January 1994, p. 44.

Gahran, Amy, "Bell Labs Saving $1.2MM with 15,000 Point BAS Installation," Energy User News, June 1994, p 26.

Gahran, Amy, "Boston Edison Pays $1.25 Million Cost of Federal Building Retrofits," Energy User News, August 1994, p 18, 41.

Gahran, Amy, "Marines Jump Procurement Hurdles to Retrofit Lighting," Energy User News, September 1994, p 1, 19.

Gilcrease, R.W., "Calculating the Energy/Environmental Benefit of a Lighting Retrofit," Strategic Planning for Energy and the Environment, Spring 1994, p. 7-12.

Gordon, J.A., "Windows Save Empire State Building $948K," Energy User News, November 1994, p. 1.

"High-Temp Superconductors Used for Energy Storage," Electric Light & Power, July 1994, p. 1.

Meckler, G., "New Directions in HVAC Systems," Energy Engineering, Volume 91, Number 2, 1994, p. 6-23.

Nelson, K.L., "Drives Retrofit Cuts Toyota Auto Body Plant's Electric Consumption 47%," Energy User News, October 1994, p 9.

Nelson, K.L., "Financed by Esco, Lighting Retrofit Saves University 2.72 MMKwh/Year," Energy User News, October 1994, p 20.

Nelson, K.L., "Hughes' T8 Retrofit in 8 Buildings Drops 5.6 MMkWh from Demand," Energy User News, August 1994, p 14.

Nelson, K.L., "School's Retrofit is Prototype for Lighting Projects in 160 Other Facilities," Energy User News, November 1994, p. 11.

Nelson, K.L., "Utility Pays for Federal Reserve Retrofits that Save 1.4 MMKWh/Yr.," Energy User News, November 1994, p. 19.

Nelson, K.L., "24 Jersey City Schools Receive Free Lighting Retrofits," Energy User News, June 1994, p 1, 16.

Randazzo, M., "Casino's New 12.25 MW Diesel Generator to Save $567,280 a Year," Energy User News, November 1994, p. 18.

Randazzo, M., "Cost Concerns Motivate Hospital Retrofit," Energy User News, October 1994, p 1, 12.

Randazzo, M., "Ecology Department Headquarters Uses 30% Less Energy," Energy User News, June 1994, p 1, 8.

Randazzo, M., "Multiphase Energy, Air Quality Project Saves Insurance Company $1.68/sq. ft.," Energy User News, September 1994, p 1, 14.

Randazzo, M., "Retrofits Cut Electricity Use by 32 MMkWh/yr," Energy User News, November 1994, p. 1.

U.S. Industrial Outlook, U.S. Department of Commerce, 1994.

Chapter 11

"Agency Slates Four Plants," Engineering News Record, September 19, 1994, p 19.

"Battelle Generates Electricity from Wood-Waste Gasification," Electric Light & Power, December 1994, p. 28.

"Big Project in Montana Planned by Private Firm," Engineering News Record, February 28, 1994, p 26.

"BPA's Large Customers Seek New Suppliers," Engineering News Record, June 6, 1994, p 21.

"Forecast Paints Promising Picture for World Power," Power Engineering, May 1994, p. 7.

Hoske, M.T., "T&D Conference Examines Global Competition," Electric Light & Power, June 1994, p. 1.

"Indian Tribes will Build Big Project Themselves," Engineering News Record, April 25, 1994, p 17.

"Lignite-Burning Plant Planned in Mississippi," Engineering News Record, September 26, 1994, p 24.

Locsin, J., "$1 Billion in Outages Planned," Electric Light & Power, December 1994, p. 21.

Loscin, J., "SCADA/EMS Study Reflects Changing Industry," Electric Light & Power, September 1994, p. 35.

"New Generating Capacity Plans Depend on Utility IRPs," Electric Light & Power, May 1994, p. 10.

Norton, F.L. and J.W. Gottlieb, "Repowering: Addressing Financial, Environmental and Regulatory Issues," presented at the World Energy Engineering Congress.

"Northwest Utility Finds Building Its Own Unit will be Less Expensive," Engineering News Record, October 3, 1994, p 25.

Reardon, R.E., "Planned Expenditures Down Sharply," Electric Light & Power, December 1994, p. 37.

"Private Market Grows Faster," Engineering News Record, April 13, 1992.

"PV System Replaces Generators at Cattle Ranch," Electric Light & Power, December 1994, p. 28.

Setzer, S.W., "Pumped Storage Job is a Rocky Challenge," Engineering News Record, March 7 1994, p. 28-29.

Smith, M., "Control System Spending Slows," Electric Light & Power, December 1994, p. 21.

Smock, R. and D. Wartentin, "Utility Capital Spending Outlook Turns Downward," Electric Light & Power, January 1995, p. 8.

Smock, R.W., "Prices Slashed 40% on New Pulverized Coal-Fired Power Plants," Power Engineering, November 1994, p. 23.

Stein, H., "Natural Gas Fuels Utility Repowering Trend," Electric Light & Power, February 1994, p. 16.

Stein, H., "Utilities Turn to Innovative Construction Technologies," Electric Light & Power, July 1994, p. 24.

Sullivan, T.M. and M.S. Briesch, "Repowering...A Ready Source of New Capacity," Presented at the 8th Cogeneration and Independent Power Congress, Boston 1993.

U.S. Industrial Outlook, U.S. Department of Commerce, 1994.

"Utilities Replace, Upgrade, Repair...To Keep Old Plants Going," Electric Light & Power, April 1994, p. 51.

Wadman, B., "Eighteenth Power Generation Survey Shows Another Record Year," Diesel & Gas Turbine Worldwide, October 1994, p. 26.

Chapter 12

"Electric Power Trends 1992," Cambridge Energy Research Associates and Arthur Andersen & Company, 1992.

"FERC Clarifies Open Access Transmission Policy," Power Engineering, July 1994, p. 6.

Hoske, M.T. and W. Beaty, "Winners will be Small Utilities, IPPs in New World of Transmission Access," Electric Light & Power, April 1994, p. 9.

"Major Changes Ahead for T&D Market, Economy," Electric Light & Power, June 1994, p. 21.

Miner, J., "Utilities Change URD Cable Practices," Electric Light & Power, July 1994, p. 16.

Reardon, R.E., "Planned Expenditures Down Sharply," Electric Light & Power, December 1994, p. 37.

Smith, D.J., "Utilities Worry About Allowing Transmission Access," Power Engineering, May 1994, p. 14.

Smock, R. and D. Wartentin, "Utility Capital Spending Outlook Turns Downward," Electric Light & Power, January 1995, p. 8.

Smock, R.W., "Access Opens to Transmission," Power Engineering, June 1994, p. 19.

Smock, R.W., "Transmission Access Continues to Open at an Accelerating Pace," Power Engineering, September 1994, p. 21.

"T&D Conference Examines Global Competition," Electric Light & Power, June 1994, p. 1.

U.S. Industrial Outlook, U.S. Department of Commerce, 1994.

Warkentin, D., "2000 Amp Power Cable Prototype Unveiled," Electric Light & Power, December 1994, p. 3.

Weiss, L., "FERC Looks Beyond EPAct," Wheeling & Transmission Monthly, January 1995, p. 1.

Chapter 13

"1993 Coal Strikes Causes Higher 1994 Production," Electric Light & Power, June 1994, p. 5.

"Clean Coal Moves Ahead on Two Fronts," Electric Light & Power, February 1994, p. 20.

"Coal Cost Drops, Generation Share Goes Up," Electric Light & Power, February 1994, p. 18.

Electric Power Monthly, Energy Information Administration, March 1994.

Energy Ventures Analysis, "Fuel Choice for New Electric Generating Capacity in the Next Century: Coal or Natural Gas," Coal Feature, 1994.

"Five-Year Low Cost Producers Still Coal-Fired," Power Engineering, January 1995, p. 3.

"Gas no Longer Fuel of Choice," Power Engineering, November 1994, p. 7.

"Gas Reserves Falling, Prices Holding," Electric Light & Power, December 1994, p. 26.

Gawlicki, Scott, M., "PFB the Next Step," Independent Energy, February 1992, p. 15.

"Low Natural Gas, Coal Prices Short-Lived," Electric Light & Power, December 1994, p. 4.

Moore, N., "1994 GasMart Revisited," World Cogeneration, September/October 1994, p. 19.

Murray, M., "Clean Coal Technology Begins to Provide the Answers," Electric Light & Power, November 1994, p. 44.

"Number of Coal Companies Declines, but Production is Booming," Electric Light & Power, April 1994, p. 48.

Rittenhouse, R.C., "National Coal Council Urges Federal CCT Incentives," Power Engineering, December 1994, p. 14.

Smith, D.J., "AFB Becomes a Viable Option for Power Generation," Power Engineering, December 1993, p. 19.

Smith, D.J., "Early PFB Operation Looks Promising," Power Engineering, December 1993, p. 12.

Smith, D.J., "Fluidized Beds Competitive with Conventional Coal-Fired Units in Electric Power Generation," Power Engineering, January 1995, p. 12.

Soast, A., "Market Shifts Call for Some Agility," Engineering News Record, 31 January 1994, p. 75.

Steffes, Dale, P.E., "A World Oil Revolution," Strategic Planning for Energy and the Environment, Fall 1994, p. 35-41.

Stein, H., "Coal Supply and Transportation Change as they Climb," Electric Light & Power, June 1994, p. 27.

Stein, H., "Gas Predicted to Increase Utility Market Penetration," Electric Light & Power, September 1994, p. 16.

Stein, H., "Natural Gas Fuels Utility Repowering Trend," Electric Light & Power, February 1994.

"The U.S. Coal Outlook and Compliance Strategies for Control of SO_2 and NOx Emissions by Electric Utilities: 1994-2000," Industrial Information Services, 1994.

"Utilities Pay More for Natural Gas than Oil," Electric Light & Power, July 1994, p. 28.

Varrasi, J., "U.S. Power Industry Retrenches," World Cogeneration, November/December 1994, p. 11.

Chapter 14

"Combined Nuclear Group Holds First Conference," Electric Light & Power, July 1994, p. 28.

Daniels, Steve, "Apaches Push Privatization," Engineering News Record, March 7, 1994, p. 8.

"Dismantling Nuclear Power Units may be Big Business -- Someday," Engineering News Record, July 18, 1994, p. 28.

Eblen, T., "End of an Era for TVA," The Atlanta Journal, 18 December 1994, p. H1.

Electric Power Monthly, Energy Information Administration, March 1994.

"Engineering Firms Join Advanced Nuclear Projects," Power Engineering, May 1994, p. 7.

Feazell, M., "Competition was the Slogan for the Nuclear industry in 1993," Waste Tech News, January 1994, p. 1.

"Fusion may be Energized," Engineering News Record, 31 October 1994, p. 10.

International Energy Outlook 1994, Energy Information Administration, 1994.

Kuehn, S.E., "Happy 15th Anniversary Three Mile Island," Power Engineering, May 1994, p. 16.

Kuehn, S.E., "Spent Fuel, Waste Issues Gaining Critical Mass," Power Engineering, October 1994, p. 14.

Kuehn, S.E., "The Least Cost Option is Nuclear Electricity," Power Engineering, January 1995, p. 11.

Locsin, J., "$1 Billion in Outages Planned," Electric Light & Power, December 1994, p. 21.

"New Mexico Apaches Agree to First MRS Site," Electric Light & Power, March 1994, p. 1.

"Nuclear Fusion Takes a Giant Step," Electric Light & Power, April 1994, p. 5.

"Nuclear Power Plant may Repower with Gas Turbines," Power Engineering, October 1994, p. 5.

Reardon, R.E., "Planned Expenditures Down Sharply," Electric Light & Power, December 1994, p. 37.

"State Regulators: Allow Private Spent Nuclear Storage," Electric Light & Power, April 1994, p. 4.

Smock, B., "Nuclear Power Reaches the Peak," Electric Light & Power, May 1994, p. 3.

Smock, B., "Action Needed on Nuclear Waste," Electric Light & Power, August 1994, p. 19.

Soast, A., "First Big U.S. Reactor Dismantled," Engineering News Record, July 18, 1994, p. 26-28.

Stein, H., "Nuclear Power's Next Generation Plants Accepted Abroad, but Approval Slow Here," Electric Light & Power, October 1994, p. 33.

"TVA Suspends Work on Three of Its Units," Engineering News Record, December 19, 1994, p. 22-23.

Chapter 15

Anderson, J.L., "Engineering Hydro's Future," Independent Energy, April 1992, p 50.

Electric Power Monthly, Energy Information Administration, March 1994.

"Hydroelectric Power Resources of the United States," Federal Energy Regulatory Commission, 1992.

Gill, H.S., "Tapping Upgrade Potential," Independent Energy, January 1993, p 60.

Hunt, R. and J.M. Hunt, "How does Hydropower Compare?" Independent Energy, November 1993, p 72.

International Energy Outlook 1994, Energy Information Administration, 1994.

Lagassa, G., "Repowering Hydro," Independent Energy, October 1992, p 46.

Soast, A., "Non-Utility Generators Offer a Growing Market," Engineering News Record, 02 December 1991, p. 23.

Chapter 16

Berenyi, E.B. and R.N. Gould, "Municipal Waste Combustion in 1993," Waste Age, November 1993, p. 51.

Charles, M.A., "New Trends in Waste-to-Energy," Waste Age, November 1993, p. 59.

Green, J.H., "Trends and Outlook for Biomass Energy," Energy Engineering, Volume 91, Number 5, 1994, p. 18-28.

"Sacramento to Build 50-MW Wind Farm," Power Engineering, July 1994, p. 6.

Soast, A., "Market Shifts Call for Some Agiligy," Engineering News Record, 31 January 1994, p. 75.

Ubaldi, R.A., "Using Waste-to-Energy to Repower Utility Electrical Generating Stations," Energy Engineering, Volume 91, Number 5, 1994, p. 66-74.

Chapter 17

"ASES Solar Report Shows the Sunny Side," Electric Light & Power, June 1994, p. 37.

Beardsley, T., "Turning Green," Scientific American, September 1994, p. 96.

"Britain Goes for Renewable Energy," Engineering News Record, April 11, 1994, p 5.

"California Boosts Wind," Engineering News Record, July 4, 1994, p 10.

"Carbonate Fuel Cells get Large-Scale Test," Engineering News Record, June 6, 1994, p. 20.

Daniels, S.H., "Wind Power Finally Coming of Age," Engineering News Record, March 28, 1994, p. 8-9.

"First Demonstration of MCFC Power Plant Technology," Power Engineering, November 1994, p. 7.

"Fuel Cell Output Breaks Record," Power Engineering, October 1994, p. 5.

"Fuel Cells Coming Into Their Own, APC Speakers Say," Electric Light & Power, June 1994, p. 34.

"Geothermal Power Takes Step Forward in Northwest," Power Engineering, December 1994, p. 5.

Gipe, Paul, "Windpower's Promising Future," Independent Energy, January 1993, p. 66.

Hunt, R. and J.M. Hunt, "How Does Hydropower Compare?" Independent Energy, November 1993, p. 72.

Kaplan, Daniel, "DoE Plans $150 Million Molten Carbonate Fuel Cell R&D Effort," The Energy Daily, Vol. 21, No. 101, May 27, 1993.

Regan, M.B., "The Sun Shines Brighter on Alternative Technology," Business Week, November 8, 1993, p. 94.

"Rural Electric Co-Op Begins Generating with Solar," Electric Light & Power, June 1994, p. 34.

"Second Army Base will Plug in Fuel Cell," Consulting-Specifying Engineer, June 1994, p. 16.

Short, William P., III, "Geothermal Status Report," Independent Energy, October 1992, p. 68.

"Southern California Edison Introduces PV Leasing Program for Remote Government, Commercial Users," Energy User News, August 1994, p. 20.

Smith, D.J., "A Growing Market for Renewable Biomass Fuels for Electric Generation," Power Engineering, December 1994, p. 16.

Stein, H., "Solar System may Break Commercial Price Barrier," Electric Light & Power, April 1994, p. 47.

"Technology Advances Rekindle Solar Power," Engineering Times, January 1995, p. 3.

Toner, M., "Breakthrough for Solar Power," Atlanta Journal, 12 November 1994, p. C1.

U.S. Industrial Outlook, U.S. Department of Commerce, 1994.

Chapter 18

Bradford, H., "Ten States to Cut Pollution," Engineering News Record, October 10, 1994, p. 10.

Bradford, H., and H. Carr, "EPA Sees NOx Rules go up a Legal Stack," Engineering News Record, December 12, 1994, p 8.

Chu, P. and B. Nott, "Field Tests Improve Knowledge About Air Toxics," Electric Light & Power, August 1994, p. 9.

"Coal-Switching will be Principal Strategy in Meeting Acid Rain Emission Requirements; EIA Finds," The Cogeneration Monthly Letter, May 1994, p. 4.

"Electric Utility Phase I Acid Rain Compliance Strategies for the Clean Air Act Amendments of 1990," Energy Information Administration, 1994.

"Environmental Externalities and Electric Utility Regulation," NARUC, October 1993.

Finnell, Janine A., "Poised for Change: The 'Greening' of Electric Utilities," Cogeneration and Competitive Power Journal, Vol. 8, No. 7, pp 48-49.

Hoske, M.T., "SO$_2$ Allowance Market Matures at Second Auction, Say Experts," Electric Light & Power, May 1994, p. 1.

"Large Study Allays EMF Fears," Engineering News Record, April 11, 1994, p 15.

"NOx Trading Begins," Electric Light & Power, June 1994, p. 5.

Smock, R.W., "SO$_2$ Allowance Market Gains Momentum in Second Auction," Power Engineering, July 1994, p. 16.

Stein, H., "Utilities Settle on Clean Air Act Compliance Plans," Electric Light & Power, August 1994, p. 15.

"The U.S. Coal Outlook and Compliance Strategies for Control of SO_2 and NOx Emissions by Electric Utilities: 1994-2000," Industrial Information Services, 1994.

"Utilities Plan Strategies For CO_2 Reduction," Electric Light & Power, June 1994, p. 4.

"Utilities Swap Credits for Stack Emissions," Engineering News Record, November 28, 1994, p. 14-15.

Chapter 19

"California School to use State's First Heavy-Duty Electric Bus," Electric Light & Power, January 1995, p. 4.

"Electric Race Cars Top 100 mph," Electric Light & Power, June 1994, p. 1.

Electric Transportation Coalition, "A New Role for Electricity as a Transportation Fuel," Strategic Planning for Energy and the Environment, Summer 1994, p. 6-10.

Electric Vehicle Association of the Americas, "SMUD and EVs: A Plan to Become the National Clean Air Capital," Strategic Planning for Energy and the Environment, Summer 1994, p. 11-13.

"EVs Exhibit Braking Stability During Tests," Electric Light & Power, January 1995, p. 4.

Hoske, M., "Electric Vehicle Batteries Advance Several Ways," Electric Light & Power, February 1994, p. 2.

Smock. R.W., "For Want of a Battery," Power Engineering, July 1994, p. 19.

Chapter 20

Annual Energy Outlook 1994, Energy Information Administration, 1994.

Annual Electric Utility Report, U.S. Department of Energy, Form EIA-861.

"Electric Power Trends 1992," Cambridge Energy Research Associates and Arthur Andersen & Company, 1992.

"Ranking of Electricity Prices: Commercial," Energy User News, October 1994, p. 56.

"Ranking of Electricity Prices: Industrial," Energy User News, November 1994, p. 46.

Smock, B., "Improving Incentives for Regulated Utilities," Electric Light & Power, July 1994, p. 5.

"Summer Rates Rose 2.2% in 1993, NARUC Says," Electric Light & Power, June 1994, p. 5.